TEAR DOWN *the* CHURCH

TEAR DOWN *the* CHURCH

THE IDEAS OF MAN VERSUS THE WORD OF GOD

Michael Huskey

AMBASSADOR INTERNATIONAL
GREENVILLE, SOUTH CAROLINA & BELFAST, NORTHERN IRELAND

www.ambassador-International.com

Tear Down the Church
The Ideas of Man Versus the Word of God

ISBN: 978-1-64960-765-2, hardcover
ISBN: 978-1-64960-637-2, paperback
eISBN: 978-1-64960-686-0

Cover Design by Hannah Linder Designs
Interior Typesetting by Dentelle Design
Edited by Jonathan Marks

Ambassador International titles may be purchased in bulk for education, business, fundraising, or sales promotional use. For information, please email sales@emeraldhouse.com.

AMBASSADOR INTERNATIONAL
Emerald House
411 University Ridge, Suite B14
Greenville, SC 29601
United States
www.ambassador-international.com

AMBASSADOR BOOKS
The Mount
2 Woodstock Link
Belfast, BT6 8DD
Northern Ireland, United Kingdom
www.ambassadormedia.co.uk

The colophon is a trademark of Ambassador, a Christian publishing company.

TABLE OF CONTENTS

ACKNOWLEDGMENT

Thank you to Steve Warner for giving me feedback on this work.

INTRODUCTION

How does the church today view weakness and dependence? What makes an individual stronger, wiser, or more capable? We will be answering these questions and many additional questions in this book. I believe that many of the views that we have today came from those who have come before us. Philosophy, secular ideology, views of church government and its purpose, doctrines of the church, theologies of the church, and practices of the church are all things that people build upon. These philosophies and practices do not materialize overnight. Many of these things have started in the past and have been added to and changed over the course of time. Often these additions and changes tend to spiral downward into error rather than bring us to a greater understanding of truth. That tendency is especially evident when we are dealing with the person and nature of God and His Church, as these have been well established in the Scriptures.

I think of the late nineteenth-century philosopher Friedrich Nietzsche's influence on our worldview. His influence has even gone beyond worldview and has been brought into the church in many ways. Maybe we should ask, "Do we, perhaps, have a view akin to Friedrich Nietzsche?" Nietzsche blamed Christianity for a weak society. He believed humility, meekness, and obedience led ultimately to civil decay because strength should be the mark of civil leadership. He taught that true fulfillment is found in being a superman (*Übermensch*). An *Übermensch* is someone who conquers his or her priorities, who conquers life, and who leads the way for others to be their own supermen. An *Übermensch* is someone who lives by his or her own wisdom. An *Übermensch* is someone who can grab the horns of life and force it to satisfy that individual's expectations. Nietzsche believed that society had derived strength from God for far too long and that God was now "dead"—people no longer believed in Him—so we must now draw our strength from within. He believed this was true for the individual, and he believed drawing strength from within was the mark of a leader. Was Nietzsche correct, or were his views simply what is built into each of us because of our individual sinful natures?

Today we seem to have a modified version of Nietzsche's worldview. We seem to have fully embraced a worldview of collectivism. "What does society believe as a whole? That is my truth," we say. Many churches seem to be motivated and influenced by the masses. They seem to find strength, wisdom, and purpose from sources outside of Scripture and those who interpret Scripture correctly. When we see people go against this strong current, they are ostracized, alienated, and deemed haters. Many churches have been influenced by this new worldview.

For us to be stronger, wiser, and more capable, do the outside influences of society need to be removed from us? For us to be stronger, wiser, and more capable, should we draw that strength from within? What about our own ideas and traditions—where do they come from? There are different ideas out there concerning each of these things. Do these ideas influence our understandings of biblical leadership and the Christian life?

When you join the military, you go through a purging of sorts called boot camp. There is an idea that to make a soldier, you need to tear down the individual first—to strip the person of everything to rebuild from a baseline and build a stronger, wiser, and more capable individual for warfare. Should this be true in the church? Should we tear down many of the ideas the church holds today to rebuild from a biblical baseline?

In my years of life, I have witnessed what Charles Spurgeon called "the downgrade." What is interesting is that this downgrade seems to be very elusive. It goes unnoticed; and for some reason, people like it that way. Many people appear to be very comfortable with the way things are. They do not want to exert much thought or energy in the kingdom of God. Anyone can slap the label "Christian" on something, and many people in the church will fully and gullibly embrace it as such. Many things are done in the name of Christ that He has no part of. Discernment has left the building, and chasing after it is unsettling because I am comfortable. Apostasy is knocking at the door; and for many, the door is already open.

This book is focused on exalting Christ in leadership, in the workplace, and in the family. In other words, in life and in ministry, Jesus Christ and the gospel should be central. We are to guard ourselves, our families, and our churches. We are to compare all things to Scripture and embrace its sufficiency. We are to examine ourselves and the truths we hold to see if those truths are absolute. We must be humble and bold enough to admit when we are wrong. Then we must strive to tear down each idea that opposes the work of Christ. Our natural desire reflects a subjective idea of the way things should be in our own minds. But we are called to a greater cause that is far beyond our natural desire. The proper understanding of this calling is found only in the closed canon, not in the subjective ideas within us nor in the collective ideas of society.

In this book, we will be pursuing that calling. We will be comparing ideas and tendencies that come from various sources to see if we have been steered off course. You will be challenged as leaders and pastors. You will be challenged in family leadership.

We will examine what things other than Scripture may influence us. We will examine the way things are to see if you are doing those things according to your ways or according to His. We will get back to the basics that have been lost in the downgrade, and I will implore you to move forward using critical thinking, examining all things according to Scripture. We will look deeper than the surface level and attempt to find the root of the things dealt with in this book. We will begin in shallow water and move into more depth by building upon each idea. I hope to first challenge you with a goal of encouraging you. So no matter if you are new to leadership and have only begun your call, or if you are a battle-scarred veteran of the faith, I pray that you will get much from this book. We will do this with the gospel leading the way because the gospel is more than our diving board; it is the ocean we swim in.

CHAPTER 1

THE FALL OF MAN AND THE CONDITION OF THE HEART

"For if while we were enemies we were reconciled to God through the death of
His Son, much more, having been reconciled, we shall be saved by His life."

Romans 5:10

"In the beginning God created."[1] These are the first words of the Holy Bible. In these words, we find that there is a relationship between two things: a Creator and a creation. In these opening words of Scripture, we see the premise and reality of who we are and who God is. There is a God and there is a creature. God sets the boundaries of the relationship that exists between Himself and all His creation. Make no mistake: all God's creations are in a relationship of some kind with Him, whether they recognize this or not. It is not always a personal relationship; creations that are not human do not relate to God personally. All people who have ever been born had a relationship with God in one way or the other—either a good relationship or a bad relationship. Paul gives us an example of this relationship with human beings in Romans 9: "You will say to me then, 'Why does He still find fault? For who resists His will?' On the contrary, who are you, O man, who answers back to God? The thing molded will not say to the molder, 'Why did you

---

make me like this,' will it? Or does not the potter have a right over the clay, to make from the same lump one vessel for honorable use and another for common use?"[2] Paul understood the Creator/creature relationship. Not only did he understand this, but he also anticipated the outrage people would have over this relationship. What causes a creature—something created—to be outraged that a Creator has the right to lord over them? It all started in the Garden of Eden.

God created all things; and when He had finished, "God saw all that He had made, and behold, it was very good."[3] This statement leaves no room for evolution. This statement leaves no room for theistic evolution. Both kinds of evolution require death, which did not exist at creation and is called an enemy of God in Scripture.[4] There was no sin; there was no death—there was simply the perfect and very good plan of God. Death is a result of sin; therefore, there was no death before the rebellion of the little creature that God had made. That creature was called Adam.

Adam was created in the image of God. What that means is that Adam was given, by God, certain attributes that God Himself possesses. This is what separated Adam from all God's other creatures: communicable attributes of God. In other words, Adam could love, be merciful, be kind, be gracious, be just, and so on, which are all attributes that God has and which He communicated to Adam through the act of creation. The communicable attributes of God are amazing gifts in themselves.

Adam was not only given these attributes—Adam was given the entire world! He was given eternal life, abundant food, paradise, a perfect and beautiful wife, but, most importantly, a good and right relationship with the very God Who created him. But God had given him something else: a truly free will. Would Adam use his free will to sustain the good relationship between himself and God, or would he choose treason?

---

2   Romans 9:19-21
3   Genesis 1:31
4   1 Corinthians 15:26

To answer this question biblically, we need to understand something. When God created the heavens and the earth, angels were also created. One of those angels was named Lucifer. Lucifer was filled with pride and believed himself to be equal with God, a fatal and foolish mistake that got him and one-third of the angels banished from Heaven because Lucifer sought to rebel against God, believing that he could rule the world better than God could rule it.[5] This insurrection happened after Adam and Eve were created and given the entire world. We know this because God said that all that He had made was "very good." It wouldn't have been "very good" if Lucifer's rebellion had happened before Adam and Eve were given the entire world.

Lucifer, also known as Satan or the serpent, now had a single and focused goal: to kill, steal, and destroy all that God had created.[6] And so, he formulated a plan to see if Adam was just like himself: a traitor. The serpent tempted Adam and Eve with the very thing that had corrupted his black soul—pride. Was it enough that Adam had the whole world? Was it enough that Adam had a perfect and beautiful wife? Was it enough that Adam had all that he could ever ask for and a good relationship with God?

God is sovereign and wanted Adam to understand that reality, so He gave Adam one rule. He placed a tree in the Garden of Eden and commanded Adam and Eve to never eat the fruit this tree bore. He told Adam that if they ate it, they would die. Satan saw an opportunity to find out if Adam and Eve would become rebels like himself. He approached Eve and said, "'You surely will not die! For God knows that in the day you eat from it your eyes will be opened, and you will be like God.'"[7] Can you see the betrayal? Can you see that this was something more than simply eating a piece of fruit? This is a question crafted by Satan to see if the world was enough or if they desired more. The only thing more would be to be God or at least like God. Were Adam and Eve

---

5   Isaiah 14:12-14; Luke 10:18; Revelation 12:4
6   John 10:10
7   Genesis 3:4-5

content with a perfect world as creatures, or did they want to be equal to the Creator? They chose treason, and they ate.

The moment that their teeth cut through the forbidden fruit, God's perfect and good creation was shattered. Death entered the world for the first time. Animals became carnivorous and began to kill and eat each other—a manifestation of the reality of death. Thorns began to grow among fruit- and vegetable-bearing plants, choking them out and creating labor for Adam and his offspring. All creation groaned in agony over the treason of Adam. But the most tragic result was that sin entered the heart of man, and the good relationship between Creator and creature became a bad relationship—an irreconcilable relationship without hope, without peace, and without life.

This was no surprise to God. God is sovereign and omniscient. He was aware that Adam would rebel. Through His sovereignty, His plan was formed before He created the earth, and that plan was to send a Messiah to be the Last Adam.[8] God Himself would embark on a rescue mission to save His elect, but what of the condition of Adam's heart? How bad would the result of Adam's treason be, and how does it affect us today?

Romans 5 tells us that a sin nature was imputed to Adam; and from Adam, all his offspring would be infected with the same sin nature. Adam acted as the federal head or representative of the entire human race. Because of his rebellion, man's heart became dark and filled with hatred; and all people who would ever be born would have a heart of stone. This is our condition. This is why Paul anticipated an outrage when he preached that God is God and man is a creature. Just as Adam wanted to be God, even as a truly free creature, so does each of us who receives from Adam a will that is only free to do what we truly want to do: treason. A free will is only free if it can choose its strongest desire; otherwise, decisions are either capricious or impossible, due to what we call "decision paralysis." The strongest desire of the human and fallen creature is to sin.

---

8   1 Corinthians 15:45

However, Jesus died to take our heart of stone and make it a heart of flesh. He died to bring us from death to life. He was the Messiah Whose mission was determined before the creation of the world. He was successful, and He is the only way to be made right before a holy God. Jesus not only was successful in His redemptive mission, but He also left behind a mission for us as His body, His Church. Jesus builds His Church through saving His elect and instructing us how to carry on His mission. That mission includes not only the responsibility of spreading the gospel into the entire world but also the edification and government of the Church.

The question we should ask is, "How much does the sin nature, passed on from Adam to us, affect the way we carry out the mission we have been given?" This is the question that every member of the body of Christ and every member in leadership should ask. Is there a part of us, as the redeemed, that still wants to be like God in the way we live, govern, preach, teach, and minister? We would never say that. We would never really want that intentionally. Yet the modern church is being run this very way. Are we the creatures who wish to be equal to the Creator? "Who are you, O man, who answers back to God?"[9]

How do we know that a Christian still struggles with a sin nature? If we struggle with sin natures, would that affect the way we live, lead, govern, and minister? Once again, we turn to Romans. In chapter 7 Paul makes this statement:

> For we know that the Law is spiritual, but I am of flesh, sold into bondage to sin. For what I am doing, I do not understand; for I am not practicing what I would like to do, but I am doing the very thing I hate. But if I do the very thing I do not want to do, I agree with the Law, confessing that the Law is good. So now, no longer am I the one doing it, but sin which dwells in me. For I know that nothing good dwells in me, that is, in my flesh; for the willing is present in me, but the doing of the good is not. For the good that I want, I do not do, but I practice the

very evil that I do not want. But if I am doing the very thing I do not want, I am no longer the one doing it, but sin which dwells in me. I find then the principle that evil is present in me, the one who wants to do good. For I joyfully concur with the law of God in the inner man, but I see a different law in the members of my body, waging war against the law of my mind and making me a prisoner of the law of sin which is in my members. Wretched man that I am! Who will set me free from the body of this death?[10]

The apostle Paul shows us in this passage that he still had a sin nature. His new nature in Jesus and his old nature were at war. Sometimes, it seemed that Paul's sin nature won a battle and influenced him in some way. If Paul, who was an apostle, struggled with this, how much more do we? Sin influences the way we interpret Scripture. That is why there are many denominations. The Bible is inerrant and infallible, but we are sinful and sometimes read our own desires into the text rather than drawing out the true meaning of the text. Sin influences the way we interact with one another in the family, in the workplace, and in the marketplace. Sin can also influence the way we govern, teach, preach, and minister in the church.

The question isn't whether we are influenced but how to identify sin's influence in our decisions. What is interesting is that, on the one hand, biblical preachers and teachers understand that we cannot earn our salvation. They know that God is the only Righteous One and that anything we do that is good comes from Him. Yet strangely, the message that comes across in most churches in America today is that you are to be strong, courageous, and the hero of your own story. This implies that strength comes from within or from some outside source, such as a non-Christian religion, secular philosophy, or general practical wisdom, that is not from God. In reality, we are to be strong in the Lord—not strong in our strength but dependent upon His.

---

10 Romans 7:14-24

In contrast to this approach, there are three things that I look for in a Christian sermon or teaching. The first thing I want to know is this: what does the text that was read say, and what does it truly mean? There is only one right interpretation of Scripture, yet there are many applications. The second thing I want to know is this: how does this text help me to understand God in a greater way? The third and final thing I want to know is this: how does this text point me to Christ? These three things are crucial; and without these three things, you will not have a fully developed Christian sermon or teaching.

Notice what I did not say. I did not say, "I want to understand how to navigate life in a better way." I did not say, "I want to hear something practical for my life." I did not say, "I want to understand how to obey the law of God in a greater way." I didn't even say, "I want to know how to apply this to my life." Scripture always, always points to Jesus Christ. Jesus is the Hero. I want and desire to know Him.

I already know and understand my own depravity, and the only solution is not found within me but within Him. I can say with confidence that the more we know Him, the more we are like Him. In other words, all those things, the practical and applicable things people want to hear, can only be found in knowing Him better, not the law, not themselves—Him. When the Key Ingredient of Christian life is absent (Christ) the practical and applicable things are just another word for law or obedience. This absence leaves behind the reality that Christ is the One Who has fulfilled these things. If Christ, the Key Ingredient, is present, then the imperatives of Scripture are clarified in terms of their intent.

The Church today is often infected by the very thing that was the downfall of Adam: wanting to do it our way. Seeking self-improvement and calling it Christianity is believing your wisdom is greater than the wisdom of Jesus. Seeking something practical or applicable, rather than seeking Him, will only leave you empty because fullness of life is found in Jesus and nothing else. So what should we focus on in the Church today? Him. If a message is preached or taught that could have been preached or taught in a synagogue, Kingdom Hall, or Church of the Latter-Day Saints, it is not a Christian message. And this is where the major problem lies in the Church today. The practical things can only be practical with Him as our Foundation, Source, and Strength. The applicable things can never be applied correctly unless Jesus Christ is the Beginning and the Ending of the law we are trying to apply.

In theological terms, I am speaking about Christocentric, rather than Christomonic teaching. Christocentric teaching and preaching focuses on proper hermeneutics to exposit and explain a text using the historical-grammatical method and then culminates that exegesis by pointing to Christ. The Christomonic method, however, will skip over exegesis and try to make all texts directly about Christ by various means, even when that flies in the face of the plain meaning of the text. For the clarity of the reader, this book is about Christocentric teaching throughout.

CHAPTER 2
PRIDE, INDEPENDENCE, AND A CAMEL NAMED CARL

"When pride comes, then comes dishonor, But with the humble is wisdom. The integrity of the upright will guide them, But the crookedness of the treacherous will destroy them."

Proverbs 11:2-3

There once was a camel named Carl. Carl's story is quite tragic because his mother died while giving birth to him. He was born in a zoo and was the only camel at the zoo after his mother's death. Carl wasn't really sure what he was. He compared himself to the lion, the zebra, and the rhino, but there was nothing like him in the zoo. Carl was kept by himself, and his only friends were the birds that visited every once in a while. As time passed, Carl began to identify as a bird. This change of identity was partly due to certain mischievous birds that convinced him that he was a bird as a cruel joke. But Carl realized he couldn't fly. However, he had seen mother birds push their young out of the nest in a tree to enable them to learn how to fly. So he became convinced that he needed a high place to jump from to learn to fly like the bird he identified as.

One day, the zoo got a new camel named Bob. Bob was placed with Carl, but Carl would have nothing to do with Bob because Bob wasn't a bird. Bob attempted, on several occasions, to convince Carl that he wasn't a bird—that he was a camel—but Carl wouldn't hear of it. In fact, he was quite offended that Bob called him a camel. He was convinced that he was a bird, and nothing could change his mind.

That night a storm blew through and tore down the gate to Carl's corral. This was his chance to escape—to find a high place and learn to fly. So Carl ran, and Bob and the birds followed, curious where he would go. He found the highest cliff just outside of town and walked to the edge. Suddenly, Bob and the birds realized what Carl was about to do, so they began to plead with him to stop. The birds didn't want Carl to die jumping from a cliff because of the cruel joke they played on him, so they told him it was all a lie. And Bob continued to reason with Carl; but Carl, once again, would not listen. Convinced that he was a bird that needed a chance to fly, Carl leaped to his death.

Carl was convinced that he was something that he obviously was not. His desire to fly like a bird overtook all his intellect and all his reasoning, and it cost him his very life. But this isn't really a story about a camel, is it? This is the reality of people who think they are something that they are not. A camel named Carl is an analogy for people convinced they are something they are not—people filled with pride.

Pride is a delusion in which an individual thinks he is something equal to or greater than his Creator. Pride blinds you; pride lies to you; pride convinces you that you are someone great. The first example of this was Lucifer. We talked about Lucifer in chapter one. We talked about how Lucifer, like Carl, believed that he was something that he was not. He believed he was as good as or even greater than God. He believed that he could overthrow God. Just as Carl leaped, believing he was a bird, Lucifer started a mutiny, believing he was like God—a very short-lived mutiny because he greatly overestimated himself. Just as Carl fell to his death, so Satan has fallen and will one day soon be cast into everlasting death.[11]

---

11   Revelation 20:10; Revelation 22:7, 12, 20.

All people have wanted to be something that they are not. The question is, from where does that desire come? Does that desire come from external or internal influences? Jesus addressed this in Matthew 15. In this chapter, Jesus uses food as an illustration. Food is something external that you place into your mouth and swallow. Sin is different; it's already in your heart from birth: "'Do you not understand that everything that goes into the mouth passes into the stomach, and is eliminated? But the things that proceed out of the mouth come from the heart, and those defile the man. For out of the heart come evil thoughts, murders, adulteries, fornications, thefts, false witness, slanders.'"[12]

In Romans 5, Paul gives us more clarity: "Therefore, just as through one man sin entered into the world, and death through sin, and so death spread to all men, because all sinned."[13] Adam sinned, receiving sin as a curse, and every person who came from Adam received that curse as well. Sin was external to Adam. But when it entered him, it infected him like a disease; and that disease became a part of the DNA of man. Carl couldn't help that he was born a camel; nevertheless, reality dictated that he was a camel. He wanted to be something else, but people (and anthropomorphic animals) cannot change the condition in which they are born. Sin is internal, not external, though it is often displayed externally. This is why the gospel is offensive. Carl was offended when Bob told him he was a camel, just like the world is offended when the gospel calls us sinners. The gospel exposes the reality of who we really are and what we desperately need. Pride is the source of our terminal disease of sin. Sin comes in many forms, yet idolatry is behind every one of them. We want to be autonomous, but autonomy is in direct conflict with sovereignty. We hate the idea of the Creator/creature relationship. God is sovereign over us, yet we crave freedom from His Lordship. We are camels who believe themselves to be birds, and that delusion could send us hurtling into everlasting condemnation.

---

12   Matthew 15:17-19
13   Romans 5:12

There is only one Lord; there is only one God; there is only one Sovereign; and there is only one Autonomous One. Sin is believing we are something that we are not. It is acting as though we are God by going against what He says we must do in Scripture. Pride is the root of sin. Pride is self-idolatry that sends us headlong into treason against a holy, sovereign, and just God. Creatures cannot obtain autonomy. We are created. Creatures naturally belong to their Creator. If we belong to someone, we cannot have autonomy. Scripture calls us slaves. We are either slaves to sin or slaves to God.

Paul tells us in 1 Corinthians 6, "Or do you not know that your body is a temple of the Holy Spirit who is in you, whom you have from God, and that you are not your own? For you have been bought with a price: therefore glorify God in your body."[14] Christians belong to God. Scripture uses the Greek word *doulos* to describe us, which means "slave." Most New Testament translations call us "bondservants," but that isn't what the Greek word *doulos* means. *Doulos* literally means "slave." We would be wise to always remember that.

On the other hand, Scripture calls those outside of Christ slaves to sin. In John 8, Jesus says, "'Truly, truly, I say to you, everyone who commits sin is the slave of sin.'"[15] We have the same problem Adam had; we want to be autonomous. We want to be free, but true freedom would be to be who the Creator created us to be, wouldn't it?

God opposes people who are prideful. Notice the emphasis here is on the people, not the action. We must see that God opposes people who are committing this action of pride. First Peter 5 tells us, "You younger men, likewise, be subject to your elders; and all of you, clothe yourselves with humility toward one another, for GOD is opposed to the proud, but gives grace to the humble." Notice this says that "God is opposed to the proud."[16] It doesn't say God is opposed to "pride"; it says, "the proud." In other words,

---

14   1 Corinthians 6:19-20
15   John 8:34
16   1 Peter 5:5

God is opposed to people who live in this delusion. God Himself is opposed to people who are proud. I call this a delusion. Pride is a delusion because it is thinking you are something when you are nothing, and the recognition of our own nothingness—our own weakness and worthlessness as sinful creatures—is what makes the gospel so beautiful because God is fully aware of our own sinfulness and saves us anyway. We don't like that God made us dependent, weak, and mortal creatures, and yet He rescues us from our own pride.

There are more consequences to having pride than being opposed by God, as if that were not enough—consequences that affect our day-to-day lives. Peter states in 1 Peter 5: "Therefore humble yourselves under the mighty hand of God, that He may exalt you at the proper time, casting all your anxiety on Him, because He cares for you."[17] Anxiety is a real problem in the fallen world in which we live. If people tell me they have never had anxiety, I will probably not believe them, because everyone that is human struggles with anxiety to one degree or another.

But this is nothing new. Sometimes, we believe that our problems are unique to us and that no one has ever struggled with the things that we do. Anxiety can be a consequence of pride or, at the very least, a lack of understanding Who God is. If you understand that God is sovereign and in control of everything that happens, then having "anxiety" shows either a lack of trust or a lack of understanding that God is sovereign. Anxiety comes from not being able to control situations that are being controlled ultimately by Him. Peter is reminding us that we should place the things that are outside of our control in the hands of the One Who is truly in control, "because He cares for you." The God who created all things "cares for you." How amazing is that?

If He "cares for you," if we can cast our anxieties on Him, then why do we choose not to? God is in control of everything, so why do we want to hang on

---

to things that are outside of our control—things that only lead us to anxiety? We want to handle things ourselves—that is the American way. We like to be in control; and when things we cannot control enter our lives, we get stressed or anxious, or we begin to worry. When people we love are out too late and we haven't heard from them, we begin to pace the floor. But do we pray? If you pray, does your anxiety leave? And if not, why does it linger?

And then there is the future. We place trust in our jobs, in our bank accounts, and in our stocks. When these things fall apart, when we lose our job or lose our money, stress and fear about tomorrow enter our minds. This can affect the way we treat our spouses, our children, our friends, and our involvement in church. What if we are in leadership—how do these things affect the way we govern and the way we teach?

R.C. Sproul once said, "If there is one single molecule in this universe running around loose, totally free of God's sovereignty, then we have no guarantee that a single promise of God will ever be fulfilled."[18] Think about that for a moment. If there were even the smallest detail in God's created universe that He did not control, then God wouldn't really be God. That probably seems asinine, but what is truly asinine is believing that we or our situations are the maverick molecule. Yet that is the way we want to act sometimes. God has given us instruction in Scripture about how we are to live and how we are to govern our churches. If we understand that the chief end of man is to glorify God and enjoy Him forever, then why do we think we should make Scripture about us? Why are pulpits filled with sermons about us rather than about God? Why do we govern the church in a way that is anything outside of what is commanded in Scripture?

A maverick molecule cannot exist at the same time and in the same place as a sovereign God. Sovereignty is our medicine for pride. God is sovereign, and it is by His grace alone that we move and have our being. Life is His creation. Who are we to think we can do things in a way that

---

18   R. C. Sproul, *Chosen by God* (Carol Stream: Tyndale House Publishers, 1986), 16.

is a single degree outside of the boundaries which He has set? When Job thought he could question God about his great worldly loss, God answered by saying:

> "Who is this that darkens counsel By words without knowledge? Now gird up your loins like a man, And I will ask you, and you instruct Me! Where were you when I laid the foundation of the earth? Tell Me, if you have understanding, Who set its measurements? Since you know. Or who stretched the line on it? On what were its bases sunk? Or who laid its cornerstone, when the morning stars sang together And all the sons of God shouted for joy? Or who enclosed the sea with doors When, bursting forth, it went out from the womb; When I made a cloud its garment, And thick darkness its swaddling band, And I placed boundaries on it And set a bolt and doors, And I said, 'Thus far you shall come, but no farther; And here shall your proud waves stop'? Have you ever in your life commanded the morning, And caused the dawn to know its place, That it might take hold of the ends of the earth, And the wicked be shaken out of it? It is changed like clay under the seal; And they stand forth like a garment. From the wicked their light is withheld, And the uplifted arm is broken. Have you entered into the springs of the sea Or walked in the recesses of the deep? Have the gates of death been revealed to you, Or have you seen the gates of deep darkness? Have you understood the expanse of the earth? Tell Me, if you know all this."[19]

God continues to chastise Job for questioning Him, yet we (unlike Job, who learned his lesson) do the same thing every day in our lives and in the Church. God has told us exactly how we are to glorify Him in all things. God has given us instruction about how to preach, teach, and govern in the Church. But we sometimes stand, as though we are in a dilution, as maverick molecules in the presence of a sovereign God when we think we have a better idea than what He has commanded. Why do we think that we are so mighty? Why do we think we can live, teach, preach, lead, and govern without poring over Scripture and praying that the Holy Spirit will lead us and guide us through our efforts at studying Scripture? Pride.

America was founded on tough and rugged men and women who pulled themselves up by their bootstraps and built this country . . . right? Isn't that the American way that we love so much? Independence is what we long for; yet when it is given, with the passing of time, some people are no longer drawn to it. America started out as a country that was focused on the freedom of the individual, and now individuals want the government to tell them what they may and may not do. Maybe in the background, those men and women who founded this country, those rugged people, were only doing what the providence of God was compelling them to do, even if their motives were not so pure. God does that after all. He causes all things to work together for good to those who love Him.

Maybe the reason, in modern America, that many people want security more than freedom now is because that is the way we were created. We were never created to be independent. We were never created to be free from God and His instructions. We were created to be dependent—to be needy, to be weak—so that we would be desperate for God. Isaiah said, "Therefore justice is far from us, And righteousness does not overtake us; We hope for light, but behold, darkness, For brightness, but we walk in gloom. We grope along the wall like blind men, We grope like those who have no eyes."[20] This is our condition on our own. This is our condition outside of Christ. We were created to grope for God, Who gives us eyes to see and ears to hear. Why do we think we can do things our way? Pride. "Who is this that darkens counsel by words without knowledge?"[21]

---

20   Isaiah 59:9-10a
21   Job 38:2

CHAPTER 3
SUPERHEROES AND GOD

"'Do not fear, for I am with you; Do not anxiously look about you,

for I am your God. I will strengthen you, surely I will help you,

Surely I will uphold you with My righteous right hand. Behold,

all those who are angered at you will be shamed and dishonored;

Those who contend with you will be as nothing and will perish.

You will seek those who quarrel with you, but will not find them,

those who war with you will be as nothing and non-existent.

For I am the Lord your God, who upholds your right hand,

who says to you, 'do not fear, I will help you.'"

Isaiah 41:10-13

When we think of superheroes, most people will have characters from their childhood come to mind, perhaps from a comic book, a television show, or a movie. Though it is true that American superheroes have been a part of our culture since 1936, other cultures have been fascinated with superheroes long before America ever existed. Herodotus wrote about superheroes over four hundred years before the time of Christ. There are early writings about Cadmus, Oedipus, Achilles, Poseidon, and many other heroes and gods of pre-Hellenistic Greek culture, who were essentially ancient superheroes. But why is there such a fascination over these fictional characters?

One reason might be that the world desperately longs for the restoration of hope. A restoration of hope is one of the things an escape into a fantasy world can bring us. Superheroes bring people hope. That is so important in a world in which hope seems to be fleeing from us. People pursue hope but never seem to be able to wrap their arms around it. It seems to be a universal Road Runner that unifies humanity on a quest to chase after it. It is faster than us and smarter than us; so we can never catch it, but we never give up. To give up would be to accept hopelessness, and life with no hope seems to be unbearable.

So we create a false sense of hope. We create objects to place our hope in such as our children, our careers, our spouses, or maybe plain ol' hedonism. Or we become like ostriches, burying our heads in the sand and pretending that all is well. We like for people to see the best of us, so we post only the best of ourselves for the world to see. Superheroes bring us hope as we turn off reality and rest in the comfort of fantasy.

Some people in the world have a desire to be rescued because they believe themselves to be victims. There is a crushing weight of desperation when they are alone. *There must be someone out there who cares. There must be a knight in shining armor for me somewhere in the world—a superhero who will rescue me from the problems that seem to bombard me,* they think. Yet as time passes—as the years click away—no superhero emerges, so they draw into themselves as a turtle into its shell in hopes of a better day.

Some people are inclined to rescue. They desire to be needed. That is what superheroes do; they rescue. So these people set out on a quest to save someone, or everyone, but from what? There are a lot of enemies to the people of the world. There are bad people, sicknesses and diseases, starvation, natural disasters, injustice, and racism and hatred. So these rescuers become police, soldiers, doctors, lawyers, crusaders, and charity-givers. But evil never ends, so ultimate fulfillment is lost.

Some people are drawn to superheroes because superheroes motivate people. These people want motivation or want to inspire motivation. There needs to be an object for them to focus on, a goal to meet or exceed. Their favorite topic is them. They love motivational books, motivational speakers, and motivational movies. Motivation is their idol because, on the inside, they are empty shells that desperately need to be filled with something, though they would never admit that.

Some people want to live as rebels. Superheroes are outside of or above the law. No one can tell a superhero what to do. In fact, superheroes tell people what to do, so those people can be safe. Superheroes control their own lives. They are outside the boundaries of normal people. They enjoy autonomy.

Some people are looking for order in a world full of chaos. The world seems like it is falling apart. Families seem like they are falling apart. Societies seem like they are falling apart. Crime seems to be out of control, and evil is prevailing. We feel a need for a savior, so we turn to a superhero as an example of how to fix all the brokenness that we see around us—someone who brings order to a world that seemed better a decade or a century ago in our minds.

A superhero can be an illusion in which we can pretend that no one can hurt us. The world is full of hurt. Life is difficult, and people are only concerned about themselves. Because of that, people hurt us. Superheroes can be bulletproof—something we wish we could be.

A superhero can illustrate our desire to be needed. We need a purpose; we need to be needed and liked while we are off to the rescue. But for some reason, no one ever gives us credit or appreciation for all that we have done for them.

The idea of becoming a superhero can be a manifestation of our fantasy about losing control. There is a certain good feeling about losing control and not being able to be stopped. There is a pleasure that comes from giving into the desire to release the rage, to crush, and to destroy. There are places where people pay money to be able to do that very thing. There is a side of us that likes letting go and letting the inner beast out. Sometimes, people take this desire too far and commit terrible crimes. Often, people only feel guilty when they are caught doing such an awful thing. There is a desire to let the inner beast out but also a desire to not face the consequences of such an action—to be a superhero who can get by with both letting out the inner beast and having no ramifications.

For some people, the idea of being a superhero can give them the fantasy of being able to disappear—to become invisible to the world and invisible to problems that life throws their way. This is particularly interesting to those of us who are introverts. When awkward situations arise, we want to disappear. When our problems become too great, we want to become invisible or intangible so nothing can hurt us. When we feel like we are not living up to the expectations of others and become ashamed of who we are or what we have done, it would be nice to be invisible so we can hide, find safety, and disappear.

For some people, the idea of becoming a superhero would be like becoming a vigilante with a sense of justice who brings justice to those who seem to deserve it. We find satisfaction in seeing things punished that we have not only been exposed to but that also seem to have slipped through the cracks of the justice system—such as wicked people that seem to get by with whatever they please. We can see an imperfect justice system and wish that there were someone, anyone, to make things right—to give people what they deserve.

That is why everyone loves superheroes, isn't it? They are people beyond the state of reality who are not weak, dependent, and mortal. Yet when we look around, we see no one seemingly worthy of such power but ourselves. The looming question is this: how did God create us to be? Why can we never seem to find fulfillment no matter what we have achieved and how good we are in the eyes of man?

The modern Church wants to be the world's superhero. Unfortunately, many local churches in America are run by people who believe themselves to be the superheroes of society, so rather than the gospel being proclaimed and being the primary driving force of the Church, social issues, which are the supervillains of society, have become front and center. These local church leaders are influential. Their congregations grow as people need something to give them purpose. They are purpose-driven superheroes who have no understanding of what the law of God is for.

In the meantime, leaders in God-centered local churches are struggling to keep their current people, much less grow. So they begin to wonder what they are doing wrong and where they can find instruction and inspiration to be like those seemingly successful congregations in town and on the television. They discover that these superhero congregations are focused on racism, feeding the poor, recycling, animal rights, feminism, and even on equal rights for homosexuals and people who are simply confused about their identity. They discover that people don't really want to be offended— what people really want is to be like the superheroes who inspire them.

Some of these things seem right, yet something is off also. So they turn to their friends in the ministry who are struggling with the same issues. They begin to go back to what they were taught in seminary by well-respected professors—well-distinguished theologians. They find that things have drastically changed over the years in seminaries across the country—that many of these seminaries are now filled with the same kind of superheroes that the seemingly successful congregations have in leadership. "Maybe this is what I have been missing," they begin to think. "Maybe I need a social platform to give people a purpose." Or perhaps they are pulled in the direction of the masses without fully realizing it. Well-loved pastors and teachers begin to jump on board this social gospel train as its conductors show, again and again, that they are not in the family of God.

Faithful congregations resist these vices. They fight against them, but their elders are getting old. They need new, young leaders to step up and lead. Many times, these new leaders have gone to these seminaries that teach anything but Christ. Many times, these new leaders have been influenced by the superheroes of the modern Church. And so, Christ begins to be less central over the course of time.

People also make superheroes out of someone who never asked for the position. There are faithful, solid pastors who have amazing personalities, who are great biblical exegetes, who shepherd well, and who are great at church government/leadership. People looking for a superhero sometimes make a hero out of this kind of pastor or teacher. Such pastors are a rare breed and deserving of respect and honor' but when the church has a mentality that they wouldn't survive if this pastor or teacher left, then who is the hero?

We should answer this question by looking at some fundamental truths about salvation. It was not Adam who sought reconciliation with God but God who sought reconciliation with Adam. From the beginning, God has been the Hero. Satan has deceived us from the beginning with three things: the lust of the flesh, the lust of the eyes, and the boastful pride of life.[22] Our desire for autonomy—our desire for what the world has to offer—is what drives us to reach for things outside of God. Sometimes, this desire can be an unnoticed cancer that begins in the most innocent kind of way until it eats, corrupts, and eventually destroys us.

The truth is that the goals and attributes of the superheroes we like are a part of the attributes of the God we deny. Hope is only found in Christ. The desire to be rescued comes from our need for a Savior, and He is right in front of you. The desire to rescue people is fulfilled in the proclamation of the gospel—the only thing that can rescue eternally. Success in the quest for motivation is found, according to Scripture, in doing what we were created to do. We were created to glorify God. To be a rebel to the ways of the world is to be found in Christ, who obeyed the law of God perfectly for us and applies that record to those of us who believe. If order is what we seek, it is only found in a sovereign God.

---

22 1 John 2:16

All Scripture points to Christ. From Genesis to Revelation, the canon of Scripture is about Him. Chris Rosebrough, a Lutheran pastor, uses the term *narcigesis* to describe the way many pastors, teachers, and churchmen read and explain their Bibles.[23] This is a fairly new term to fit a new description of a method of interpreting Scripture. Two of the more common terms would be *exegesis*, meaning "drawing the true meaning out of Scripture," and *eisegesis*, which means "reading your own opinion, doctrine, or theology into the text."

Narcigesis would be different from either of these. The prefix "narci-" comes from "narcissist" or "narcissism," the second of which means that you think the world revolves around you. It is the apex of pride. If you think the world revolves around you, you are a narcissist. Narcigesis would be the act of reading yourself into the story of the Bible, believing that it is all about you. You are the hero of the story. Narcigesis seems to be a key characteristic of the bulk of sermons preached in America today. In sermon preparation, more time is often used to find a relatable story to tell to draw people in than is used in explaining Scripture.

People are looking for a superhero. They want something practical preached so that they can better obey. They want a superhero preaching to aspiring superheroes. Application supersedes biblical exposition. The preacher is a superhero because he is preaching what people want to hear. The people are superheroes because now they know what to do. All the while, Jesus stands in a dark corner of the room with dust on His head, grieving. His name is mentioned every once in a while to make sure people know they are in a church instead of a motivational seminar.

Does this remind you of any of the churches in chapters two and three of the book of Revelation? Jesus said that the church in Ephesus had "left

---

23   Chris Rosebrough, "Narcigesis," in *Fighting for the Faith*, December 7, 2012, podcast, MP3 audio, 2:07:45, https://crosebrough.typepad.com/fightingforthefaith/2012/12/narcigesis.html.

their first love."[24] He said that some people in the church at Pergamum were "holding the teaching of Balaam."[25] He said to Thyatira, "I have this against you, that you tolerate the woman Jezebel, who calls herself a prophetess, and she teaches and leads My bond-servants astray so that they commit acts of immorality and eat things sacrificed to idols."[26] Jesus said to Sardis, "I know your deeds, that you have a name that you are alive, but you are dead."[27] And Jesus said to Laodicea, "I know your deeds, that you are neither cold nor hot; I wish that you were cold or hot. So because you are lukewarm, and neither hot nor cold, I will spit you out of My mouth."[28]

These warnings from Christ are still true today. Have you lost your first love? Are you holding teachings found outside of Scripture? Are you sympathetic to immorality and idolatry? Does your church have a name and reputation for being alive, despite being dead? Or have you become completely useless to Christ and will be spit from His mouth? These questions can be answered with two more questions: who is your hero? And how does that affect everything in your ministry and everything in your life?

---

24   Revelation 2:4
25   Revelation 2:14
26   Revelation 2:20
27   Revelation 3:1
28   Revelation 3:15-16

CHAPTER 4
PEOPLE OF DUST

"Then the Lord God formed man of dust from the ground,
and breathed into his nostrils the breath of life; and man became a living being."

Genesis 2:7

God took dust from the ground and created mankind. Without God forming us and breathing life into us, we would still be dust. There would be no life. We would do well to remember that. To understand that we are people of dust is to understand humility, to find appreciation, and to find purpose in this life. When the reality of who we are is forgotten or sensationalized, humility, appreciation, and purpose are lost. We become like the lunatic who believes he can grasp the wind in his hand to control it. We are so easily distracted.

When clarity about who we are is lost, we search for identity in other things. We become defined by identity or identify in ways that are counterproductive. At that point, we begin to struggle because there is no such thing as identity outside of Christ. He determines our identities. As an example, one of the things that Christians often struggle with is joy. This is especially true in church leadership. Joy is lost because we believe that we deserve something better than what God has given to us—something better than the way He created us. Joy was lost in the garden and can now only be found in Christ. When you believe that joy is found in recognition, good

health, obedience, or tangible things, then you will never be able to wrap
your hands around it, like the lunatic grasping the wind.

As another example of this problem, think about the idea of self-image in
America. That is really what drives our society, isn't it? When we turn on the
television, we are told that we deserve some shiny new object. Self-esteem is
spewed at us from what seems like every angle and person in life because we
are important people, we are strong, we are courageous, and we are capable.
We end up believing it. The result of this ideology is a sense of emptiness, of
loneliness, and of never achieving the dreams and accomplishing the goals
that we have set for ourselves. Yet when we learn this, we set our course to
be corrected (until tomorrow, that is). When tomorrow comes, we chase the
ghosts of the past.

It seems we never learn because it isn't in our hearts. We must be
reminded again and again that this life isn't about us; yet often, when we
go to church, we are told that it is. Change must be made by leadership or in
leadership itself if this is the case, for it is time for judgment to begin with the
household of God.[29] Perhaps it is from the pew that this message of inflated
self-esteem is proclaimed as people tell their leaders that they want to hear
the same messages in the church that they hear in the world, and therefore,
our leaders need to do a better job of holding their people accountable for
their false beliefs.

We are people of dust. James says it well: "Come now, you who say, 'Today
or tomorrow we will go to such and such a city, and spend a year there and
engage in business and make a profit.' Yet you do not know what your life
will be like tomorrow. You are just a vapor that appears for a little while and
then vanishes away."[30] We are people of dust created for a purpose outside of
this visible, tangible physical world—a purpose that is only revealed on the

---

29   1 Peter 4:17
30   James 4:13-14

pages of Scripture. Life is a vapor; it is a dot on the surface of time. But what happens in this dot means everything. Then what is the purpose of life?

James continues: "Instead, you ought to say, 'If the Lord wills, we will live and also do this or that.' But as it is, you boast in your arrogance; all such boasting is evil. Therefore, to one who knows the right thing to do and does not do it, to him it is sin."[31] What is the first thing this tells us? Every decision in this life should be made according to the will of the Lord. What is the will of the Lord? I really like what the Westminster Shorter Catechism says: "Question: what is the chief end of man? Answer: man's chief end is to glorify God and to enjoy Him forever."[32][33]

Notice that there are two parts to this answer. The last part—to enjoy God—rolls off the first—to glorify God. This really sums up the Lord's will: that we glorify Him. Our chief purpose in life is to glorify God. This is accomplished by worship, prayer, adoration, proclamation of the gospel, proclamation of the Word of God, teaching, instruction, reproof, and obedience. These are all birthed out of the gospel. The gospel isn't our diving board; it is the ocean we swim in. In other words, our whole purpose starts with Christ, and our whole purpose is fulfilled in Christ. We worship Him because of Who He is and what He has done for us. We pray to Him because of Him; we adore Him because of Him; we teach about Him because of Him; we correct because of Him; and we obey because of what He has done and because of who He has made us to be. We are image-bearers of God. And when we live this way—and only when we live this way—can we enjoy Him forever.

"But as it is, you boast in your arrogance; all such boasting is evil."[34] The chief end of man is to glorify himself and enjoy life in the moment, according to the catechism of the world. Yet it is the apex of arrogance to

---

31 James 4:15-17
32 Orthodox Presbyterian Church, *The Westminster Confession of Faith and Catechisms with Proof Texts* (Willow Grove: Orthodox Presbyterian Church, 2007).
33 Psalm 86:9; Isaiah 60:21; Romans 11:39; 1 Corinthians 6:20, 10:31; Revelation 4:11; Psalm 16:5-11, 144:15; Isaiah 12:2; Luke 2:10; Philippians 4:4; Revelation 21:3-4
34 James 4:16

believe that you are smarter, wiser, and more knowledgeable about how to live life than God is, giving you the right to live outside of what God has instructed. Do you believe you can better minister to people if you are more relatable to them? Do you believe that to grow a church, you must be more like the world so that they will be attracted to Jesus? Jesus doesn't want your arrogance, and He doesn't need you to make Him look good. This is the true reason there are so many disagreements in theology: the quest to make Jesus look good—the idea that Jesus must be fair and exactly the way that you want Him to be in your own mind. You don't want Jesus to be fair (since that would mean you would be condemned to Hell for being a rebellious sinner); and when you make Him to be the God you like, that is idolatry. The only thing that would be fair for us is judgment. That is what we deserve, yet God gives some of us mercy.

Jesus is King of kings and Lord of lords.[35] Jesus is omnipotent. He is all-powerful. He possesses every ounce of power in the universe; and there is no person, no angel from Heaven or demon from the bottomless pit, nor anything that can overthrow Him. He is mighty. He is unlimited in power and strength, and nobody can usurp Him. We serve not only a powerful God but also a God Who is the Issuer of power to anyone or anything that has any power at all. In other words, He is the Source of all power in the universe; and anything that we can think of that has any power at all only gets that power from God Himself because He has spoken it. We find comfort in this, don't we—an omnipotent God Whose "power" is "toward us who believe"?[36] If God is for us, who can be against us? Understanding this not only helps us know God and Who He is but it also helps us understand the "power" behind what we do when we are walking in His will.

Jesus is no longer dead; He is resurrected. Jesus went to the cross for you. He died for you. And God the Father raised Him to show us that His death was

---

35   See Ephesians 1:19-21 and Revelation 19:16.
36   Ephesians 1:20

not in vain. His death was successful. His death accomplished the redeeming work you need if you want to stand before God one day and be innocent. You will stand before Him. You will either stand guilty or you will stand covered by His blood. Jesus is seated at the right hand of the Father because He is God![37] He is "far above all rule and authority and power and dominion, and every name that is named."[38] Jesus is "far above . . . Every name that is named"—not just today, not just tomorrow, but for all eternity. Paul said in Ephesians, "And He put all things in subjection under His feet, and gave Him as head over all things to the church, which is His body, the fullness of Him who fills all in all."[39] God put everything "under Jesus's feet." He is supreme.

In the book of Revelation, Jesus is shown to have feet of bronze. The altar in the Old Testament was made of bronze. This is where the priests made daily sacrifices to atone for the sins of the people. Jesus fulfilled the sacrificial system at the cross. To be reminded of the supremacy of Christ, look at Revelation 1:13-17:

> I saw one like a son of man, clothed in a robe reaching to the feet, and girded across His chest with a golden sash. His head and His hair were white like white wool, like snow; and His eyes were like a flame of fire. His feet were like burnished bronze, when it has been made to glow in a furnace, and His voice was like the sound of many waters. In His right hand He held seven stars, and out of His mouth came a sharp two-edged sword; and His face was like the sun shining in its strength. When I saw Him, I fell at His feet like a dead man.[40]

Do you see Him? Are you following His ways? Jesus isn't a baby anymore. Jesus isn't a white guy with long blond hair walking around holding a sheep. When John "saw Him," he "fell at His feet like a dead man."[41] What is your

37 Ephesians 1:19
38 Ephesians 1:21
39 Ephesians 1:22-23
40 Revelation 1:13-17
41 Revelation 1:17

reaction? Have you really seen Christ, or do you just like the idea of Him? In your ministry and in your life, do you live as though you have seen Christ?

This isn't the last time that John would see Jesus like this. John sees Jesus again:

> And I saw heaven opened, and behold, a white horse, and He who sat on it is called Faithful and True, and in righteousness He judges and wages war. His eyes are a flame of fire, and on His head are many diadems; and He has a name written on Him which no one knows except Himself. He is clothed with a robe dipped in blood, and His name is called The Word of God. And the armies which are in heaven, clothed in fine linen, white and clean, were following Him on white horses. From His mouth comes a sharp sword, so that with it He may strike down the nations, and He will rule them with a rod of iron; and He treads the wine press of the fierce wrath of God, the Almighty. And on His robe and on His thigh He has a name written, "KING OF KINGS, AND LORD OF LORDS."[42]

This is the supremacy of Christ. Jesus is "King of kings and Lord of lords"; do you know Him? Jesus is Head over the church. The pope isn't the head of the church, nor is any pastor. Jesus is Head over the Church. There is no mere man who is head over the Church, and we would be wise to understand two things that are related to this truth. First, we must understand that God is over His Church. Second, we must understand that we must humbly submit to His authority. Jesus is omnipotent, and He is coming in judgment against all those who are not in Him. As frightening as an omnipotent God is, it is also the most comforting thing to understand that He loves us. He watches over us. He guides us. If we are not in His will, that guidance takes the form of discipline.

We are people of dust who have been given a mission by the King of Kings and Lord of Lords. Will you follow Him, or will you follow the ways the professionals tell you that you should do things? Will you humbly submit to His authority? If so, it is time to start getting serious about ministry; and it is time to start getting serious about life as an image-bearer of God. Getting serious means that we take the Bible as the sole authority in the Church. We, as the Church, are to be what Scripture instructs us to be. In our local churches, we do not have the authority to play God and change things to be more palatable, even if that is what is happening in other congregations and even if that is what is being taught in many seminaries. We do not look at the ways of people. We look to, trust in, and strive to be faithful to what God has commanded us to do in ministry and in life. I will leave you with the words of John Calvin:

"It is evident that man never attains to a true self-knowledge until he has previously contemplated the face of God, and come down after such contemplation to look into himself. For (such is our innate pride) we always seem to ourselves just and upright, and wise, and holy, until we are convinced, by clear evidence, of our injustice, vileness, folly, and impurity. Convinced, however, we are not, if we look to ourselves only, and not to the Lord also—He being the only standard by the application of which this conviction can be produced. For, since we are all naturally prone to hypocrisy, any empty semblance of righteousness is quite enough to satisfy us instead of righteousness itself. And since nothing appears within us or around us that is not tainted with very great impurity, so long as we keep our mind within the confines of human pollution, anything which is in some small degree less defiled delights us as if it were most pure."[43]

43   John Calvin, *Institutes of the Christian Religion*, trans. Henry Beveridge (Peabody: Hendrickson Publishers, 2008), Book 1, Chapter 2.

CHAPTER 5

How the Law of God and the Gospel Work Together in Redemption and Sanctification

"Sanctification is that inward spiritual work which the Lord Jesus Christ works in a man by the Holy Spirit, when He calls him to be a true believer. He not only washes him from his sins in His own blood, but He also separates him from his natural love of sin and the world, puts a new principle in his heart and makes him practically godly in life."[44]

I find it interesting that all biblical Christian denominations would with one voice proclaim that obeying the law of God can save no one. Yet in most churches in America today, the gospel is entirely absent from the message preached from behind the pulpit. Instead, churches are filled with moralistic therapeutic deism that gives the churchgoer the following two ideas: that obedience earns salvation and that the gospel will help you feel good about yourself. Morality is preached as though hope is found in morality alone. Many people have low self-esteem and want to hear a positive message so they can be revitalized for the week ahead. God is looked at as though He is far removed from His creation and has given total sovereignty to the creature.

---

44 J. C. Ryle, *Holiness: Its Nature, Hindrances, Difficulties, and Roots* (London: James Clark and Co., Limited, 1952), 15.

If this kind of preaching is prevalent, don't we lose what makes Christianity different from all other religions in the world? What separates the true religion from all false religions is that salvation cannot be earned. What separates what we believe from what they believe is the Christian declaration that you are an enemy of God and have no hope without Christ. The gospel is offensive. What separates us from all false religions is that our God is omnipresent, sovereign, omnipotent, loving, just, and immutable. In other words, He isn't like us. We simply have some of His communicable attributes that He was gracious enough to share with us. Why could most sermons in America today be preached at the Kingdom Hall, Church of Latter-Day Saints, or the synagogue?

The reason is partially our own fault and partially the work of our enemy. We need to understand the reality that Satan is good at what he does. One of his favorite things to do is to confuse people about what is declared in Scripture. That is what he has done from the very beginning when he twisted God's Word in the garden. The answer to why many sermons in the church today could be preached in a heretical denomination is that many sermons today are missing a proper view of the law of God. Pastors think that the law of God is something we can follow on our own, but this thought is unbiblical. The law of God was given to mankind to show us who we really are.

Scripture reveals our identity very clearly. Ephesians 2:1 tells us, "You were dead in your trespasses and sins." Ephesians 2:3 tells us we were "by nature children of wrath."[45] Romans 5 calls us enemies of God.[46] Colossians 1 says we were "alienated and hostile."[47] Genesis 6 says, "The Lord saw that the wickedness of man was great on the earth, and that every intent of the thoughts of his heart was only evil continually."[48] Jeremiah tells us, "The heart is more deceitful than all else And is desperately sick; Who can understand

---

45   Ephesians 2:1-3
46   Romans 5:10
47   Colossians 1:21
48   Genesis 6:5

it?[49] Scripture makes a charge against mankind, and the way we understand that charge is by the law of God.

The law of God is summarized in the Ten Commandments. James tells us in chapter two that "whoever keeps the whole law and yet stumbles in one point, he has become guilty of all."[50] The law of God is a perfect unity. To break just one law ever in your life is to break every single one of them. That is because the act of breaking the law of God exposes something about you. Jesus helps us understand what is exposed when we break one law of God.

Matthew writes, "A lawyer asked Him a question, testing Him, 'Teacher, which is the great commandment in the Law?' And He said to him, 'YOU SHALL LOVE THE LORD YOUR GOD WITH ALL YOUR HEART, AND WITH ALL YOUR SOUL, AND WITH ALL YOUR MIND. This is the great and foremost commandment. The second is like it, 'YOU SHALL LOVE YOUR NEIGHBOR AS YOURSELF.'"[51] The reason that to be guilty of breaking one law of God is to be guilty of breaking them all is because the act of breaking the law of God exposes that we do not love God. In other words, we have something we love more than God—our own ways.

The law of God was never meant to save you; it is meant to show you that you are incapable of keeping it. God's law is meant to point you to the Savior. Even though we are in Christ, we fail to keep Christ's commandment to love God. We can always conceive of being able to love God in a greater way. But in Christ, our sin of failing to love God properly (along with all our other sins) is propitiated.

The Law will not change you—that is one of the most fundamental doctrines of the Christian faith—yet we focus so much of our efforts on morality, application, or something practical when we should be focused on Jesus. He is the One Who changes you. Know Him, and you will be humbled. Know Him, and you will be changed. Know Him, and He will guide

---

49   Jeremiah 17:9
50   James 2:10
51   Matthew 22:35-39

you through this life. We are going to flesh this out more when we get to chapter eleven: "Obligations of Leadership in the Church." Here is a preview: obedience must be birthed out of the gospel. Practical and applicable things are not possible outside of the gospel. Both law and gospel should be a part of every teaching labeled *Christian* without exception.

It may be unintentional for pastors to preach morality over Christ. In many local churches, morality is a badge of honor. I have heard people say they go to a certain local church because the pastor isn't afraid to preach against homosexuality and other acts of sexual immorality. I have heard people say they attend their local church because the pastor preaches against drinking alcoholic beverages. They go to these local churches because their pastors tell them to be better, work harder, and be more like Jesus. They love to be told to do this and to not do that, but where is Christ? Or maybe these people love the fact that the person across the aisle is hearing this message because they themselves are already being obedient to God. Some sermons today assume that the gospel is understood by every person in the room, so their focus becomes other things. In reality, those other things should only flow from the gospel as logical consequences of a prior understanding of the gospel. The gospel must be central. Obedience preached with no gospel is a false message that can be heard at any meeting of apostates. Obedience with no gospel is the false religion of the world.

Obedience with no gospel produces confidence in a false god. There is nothing more dangerous to the church than religious confidence in a fake god of our own imagination. As an example, in the second century, a man named Marcion believed that the God of the Old Testament was different from the God of the New Testament, so he famously reduced the Bible to just the gospel of Luke and ten letters of Paul. He is one of the reasons that the church had to universally agree that our canon of Scripture is accurate. Marcion didn't like the God of the Old Testament because he believed that the God of the Old Testament was wrathful. He liked the God of the New

Testament better because he saw the God of the New Testament as a God of love. Marcion created a God of his own liking. He created an idol using biblical ideas, just like all cults and some mainstream churches do today.

What is the solution to this problem? The pastor's job in the church is to preach the whole counsel of God. The father in the home is responsible to teach his family the whole counsel of God also. Both responsibilities require proper hermeneutics. What I mean by that is that we must teach what Scripture is pointing to, no matter what passage we are in. All Scripture is either directly or indirectly about Christ. If you are teaching from the Old Testament, the text is pointing to Christ. If you are teaching from the New Testament, the text is about Christ. It doesn't matter whether you are a topical teacher or a verse-by-verse teacher—true hermeneutics and Christian teaching will always point us to Jesus. Law without Christ is a false idol. Law without the gospel brings a false security in the flesh. Law without pointing to Christ gives us a false image of God and a false gospel and a false god altogether.

Martin Luther wrote:

> For if I were to teach men the Law in such a way that they suppose themselves to be justified by it before God, I would be going beyond the limit of the Law, confusing these two righteousnesses, the active and the passive, and would be a bad dialectician who does not properly distinguish. But when I go beyond the old man, I also go beyond the Law. For the flesh or the old man, the Law and works, are all joined together. In the same way the spirit or the new man is joined to the promise and to grace. Therefore when I see that a man is sufficiently contrite, oppressed by the Law, terrified by sin, and thirsting for comfort, then it is time for me to take the Law and active righteousness from his sight and to set forth before him, through the Gospel, the passive righteousness which excludes Moses and the Law and shows the promise of Christ, who

came for the afflicted and for sinners. Here a man is raised up again and gains hope.[52]

Luther brings up an interesting point: there are two righteousnesses—active and passive. What he calls *active righteousness* is a person actively attempting to achieve righteousness by obeying the law of God. What he calls *passive righteousness* is a person passively receiving righteousness by imputation from Christ. Luther is talking about a man who has tried and failed at obeying the law of God and has become terrified by sin because he understands that he cannot obey the law. He is convicted of his sins because he understands that God is holy and just. Luther points the man to Christ's imputed righteousness through the gospel. Jesus obeyed the law of God for His elect; Jesus imputes His active righteousness upon us; and Jesus makes us righteous through that act of imputation. This is a passive act by us because we did not earn it. This was an active act by Christ because He achieved it.

I have mentioned the imputed righteousness of Christ but haven't yet defined this amazing doctrine. This is one of the most important doctrines that we should understand and one of the most overlooked and misunderstood doctrines. Imputation is a doctrine that can help us to understand the law of God and the gospel in a greater way. One of the best passages to unpack this doctrine is found in Romans 5:12-14.

Paul begins by showing us that a sin nature is passed from Adam to all people who would ever be born: "Therefore, just as through one man sin entered into the world, and death through sin, and so death spread to all men, because all sinned—for until the Law sin was in the world, but sin is not imputed when there is no law. Nevertheless death reigned from Adam until Moses, even over those who had not sinned in the likeness of the offense of Adam, who is a type of Him who was to come."[53] This text

52   Martin Luther, "Lectures on Galatians Chapters 1-4," in *Luther's Works*, eds. Jaroslav Pelikan and Walter A. Hansen (St. Louis: Concordia Publishing House, 1963), p. 6-7.
53   Romans 5:12-14

shows us the imputation of sin from Adam ("one man") to all men.[54] All men sinned in Adam. Verse thirteen says, "For until the Law sin was in the world." Sin was in the world from Adam until the Law of Moses was given and has been in the world since that time. Sin was in the world even though there was no law. "But sin is not imputed when there is no law."[55] What does the word *imputed* mean? The Greek word is *ellogeo* (el-lo-ge-ō), which is an accounting term. It means to reckon, set to one's account, or lay to one's charge.[56] This sets up what is said in verse fourteen: "Nevertheless death reigned from Adam until Moses, even over those who had not sinned in the likeness of the offense of Adam." How did "death reign from Adam until Moses" if there was no Law? Paul wants us to understand something. Sin was "imputed" to all Adam's offspring—Christ being the only exception.

We are each born with sin natures that corrupt what we desire. There was only one law before Moses, and that was to not eat of the tree of knowledge. After Adam and Eve partook, they were banished from the garden and no longer allowed access to that tree, yet people continued to die. "The wages of sin is death."[57] The reason people died between Adam and when the Law was given to Moses on Mount Sinai is because sin was imputed to all people born of Adam. Jesus clarifies the imputation of sin in Mark 7:14-23:

> After He called the crowd to Him again, He began saying to them, "Listen to Me, all of you, and understand: *there is nothing outside the man which can defile him* if it goes into him; but the things which *proceed out* of the man are what defile the man. [If anyone has ears to hear, let him hear."]

> When He had left the crowd and entered the house, His disciples questioned Him about the parable. And He said to them, "Are

---

54   Romans 5:12
55   Romans 5:13
56   James Strong, *A Concise Dictionary of the Words in the Greek Testament and the Hebrew Bible* (n. p: n.d.), 1:27, s.v. "ellogeo."
57   Romans 6:23

you so lacking in understanding also? Do you not understand that whatever goes into the man from outside cannot defile him, *because it does not go into his heart,* but into his stomach, and is eliminated?" (Thus He declared all foods clean.) And He was saying, *"That which proceeds out of the man, that is what defiles the man.* For from within, out of the heart of men, proceed the evil thoughts, fornications, thefts, murders, adulteries, deeds of coveting and wickedness, as well as deceit, sensuality, envy, slander, pride and foolishness. All these evil things proceed *from within* and defile the man" (emphasis mine).[58]

We are not sinners because we sin. Scripture teaches that we sin because we are sinners. Sin is inside of us because we are descendants of Adam. We are imputed his rebellion as though we rebelled against God ourselves. We will choose to do what our strongest desire is, and what our strongest desire is, unless we believe in Christ, is to sin.

The doctrine of imputation is both the most tragic and the most beautiful doctrine in all Scripture. Adam is a type of Jesus Christ. Adam was the federal head of the entire human race. He was our representative. Jesus is the Last Adam, which tells us that He is also representing a group of people as their federal Head. Paul tells us in 1 Corinthians 15, "So also it is written, 'The first MAN, Adam, BECAME A LIVING SOUL.' The last Adam *became* a life-giving spirit. However, the spiritual is not first, but the natural; then the spiritual. The first man is from the earth, earthy; the second man is from heaven. As is the earthy, so also are those who are earthy; and as is the heavenly, so also are those who are heavenly."[59]

Just as Adam represented the entire human race by his disobedience to God, so Jesus, the Last Adam, represents all His elect by His obedience to God. This is the greatest news the world has ever been given. Jesus Christ Himself took on the nature of man to be our new Representative. Paul says elsewhere, "The

58   Mark 7:14-23
59   1 Corinthians 15:45-48

gift is not like that which came through the one who sinned; for on the one hand the judgment arose from one transgression resulting in condemnation, but on the other hand the free gift arose from many transgressions resulting in justification."[60] Adam gave the gift of condemnation; Christ gave the gift of redemption resulting in justification. It took one sin to curse the entire world. Yet millions upon millions of sins were aimed at God, and they were all laid upon Christ at the cross. He is the only One Who could endure this. This is why it had to be Jesus. Only God Himself could take the weight of this. This is what penal substitutionary atonement means.

"For if by the transgression of the one, death reigned through the one, much more those who receive the abundance of grace and of the gift of righteousness will reign in life through the One, Jesus Christ."[61] The grace of God is abundant. There is no sin that is too great for the grace of God. There are not too many sins to be covered by the blood of Christ. It is never too late to fall at His feet and cry for mercy, if a person is still alive. The fact that righteousness is a gift shows that it cannot be earned. There is nothing that we can do to be pleasing or impressive to God. Righteousness is not of ourselves; our only possible righteousness is the righteousness of Christ. We are made righteous "through the One, Jesus Christ." Those who belong to Christ are in Christ. When God looks upon us, He sees Jesus. This is why we "reign in life."

The next two verses solidify the imputation of righteousness from Christ: "So then as through one transgression there resulted condemnation to all men, even so through one act of righteousness there resulted justification of life to all men. For as through the one man's disobedience the many were made sinners, even so through the obedience of the One the many will be made righteous."[62] Though Adam's sin was imputed to all people who have ever or will ever live, Christ Jesus imputed His righteousness to those who believe.

---

60   Romans 5:16
61   Romans 5:17
62   Romans 5:18-19

This is sometimes called "the sweet exchange." The sin imputed to us from Adam can now be imputed to Christ, and Jesus's righteousness can now be imputed to you, if you will only believe.

It is our understanding of what Christ has done for us that drives us deeper into the meatier truths of God's Word. It is the gospel that changes us. No program will change you. No class, no psychologist, and no amount of counseling will change you unless it (or the person) is rich in the gospel. This is why we desperately need the gospel every day. "The Law came in so that the transgression would increase; but where sin increased, grace abounded all the more."[63] Remember that there was sin and death before "the Law came in." Why did the law come in? "So that the transgression would increase."

In other words, God wanted to be very clear that we cannot be saved by obeying the law. God increased our understanding of both His amazing work and our desperate need for a Savior by giving us the law. This is merciful. This is kind. This is loving. Imagine what it would mean if God had never given us the understanding that we cannot obey our way to eternal life. But He graciously made it clear that we cannot be saved by obedience to the law. Because our understanding of our own depravity was increased by the giving of the law, our understanding of what amazing grace has been poured out upon us should also increase. The more you understand your own depravity, the more you will glorify God because of what He has done for you by saving you through the sacrifice of Christ; and you will also glorify God for His work in your sanctification.

We also must be careful to not be antinomian or against God's law. The law of God isn't thrown out the window because it is fulfilled in Christ. For the lost, the law of God exists so that they understand that it is impossible to keep and that they need a Savior to obey it perfectly. For believers, we have righteousness imputed to us by Christ; and now the law of God is a standard

---

we strive for. We don't do this to earn salvation but because we love Christ. We have been given a new heart by Him, and now we want to be as much like Christ as we possibly can be. The law of God is holy and good, and we should cherish it as believers.

A Christian sermon, one that cannot be preached in a Kingdom Hall, Church of Latter-Day Saints, or synagogue, must have both law and gospel. People need to understand that they have offended a holy God and that a price must be paid for their betrayal. They must understand that Jesus is truly God and truly human. He had to be truly human to pay for the sins of people. He had to be truly God to propitiate or satisfy the Father. He had to be truly God to pay the cost of a sin against an eternal, infinite God. If a sermon isn't pointing us to Christ, then it is a failure. It isn't a Christian sermon, and it isn't pleasing to God. It brings confusion and disunity to the body of Christ, and it should be called out by discerning people as a source of confusion and disunity.

I see a source of great confusion behind the pulpit today. Many, out of one side of their mouths, say that the law cannot save you; yet they preach obedience out of the other side. They do this with no mention of Jesus fulfilling the law for us. They teach that we are overcomers because we overcome sin rather than because Christ has overcome it for us. We are overcomers because Jesus gives us the power to not sin rather than because we are in Him who has no sin. Is this view a good representation of freedom? It would be an empowered freedom, fueled by Christ.

We are free if we have fuel to keep our heads above water. We are the ones doing the swimming with Christ as our fuel. Without Christ giving us fuel, we would sink back into the slavery of sin and death. That may sound right on the outside, but there is neither assurance nor freedom in a view like that one. This idea teaches that we are in sin rather than in Christ, that there is no fundamental difference between the believer and the unbeliever, and that salvation doesn't really change us at the most fundamental level.

On the outside, it may sound right to emphasize that Jesus gives us the power to not sin; however, there is no assurance in a view like that because Scripture tells us that we were, by our very natures, slaves to sin. If Christ does not fundamentally change us, we remain in sin. If you hold to the view that Christ gives us the power to not sin but does not change us in any other way, you must embrace being in sin rather than being in Christ. Jesus is not merely an outside Force to help you not sin. A believer is not in sin but in Christ. The yoke of the law is not a burden that we can be empowered to bear; rather, we take the yoke of the law off, and we put on the yoke that is light and easy to bear.[64]

It is true that we have the power of the Holy Spirit that helps us overcome sin, and we should understand that. It is also true that the believer is in Christ and is viewed as being righteous because of His great sacrifice. Understand that there is a big difference between being in sin and given the power to overcome, on the one hand, and being in Christ and overcoming because He is the Overcomer, on the other hand.

Scripture teaches that we are in Christ. It is as though we have been submerged into Him. He is all-consuming. The believer is in Christ, not in sin, because of imputed righteousness. We have sin natures, but we are not in sin; we are in the state of justification because we are in the One Who justifies. A failure to understand this is a failure to understand Christian theology.

One of the reasons that Christian theology is not understood is because we keep repeating the same mistakes of the past—mistakes that other Christians have already dealt with and addressed in Church history. "No creed but Christ" sounds nice, but it diminishes the reality that God has given us teachers as a blessing to the Church and the reality that He has given us Scripture. It is true that Scripture is our only authority. It is true that the canon of Scripture is closed and that we cannot add to or take away from it. But it is also true that God has given, as a gift, faithful teachers in every age to

---

64 Matthew 11:28-30

proclaim the truths of Scripture. And to refuse to learn from faithful teachers of God's Word from the past is a significant mistake. Scripture makes clear that God gives us teachers:

> And He [God] gave some as apostles, and some as prophets, and some as evangelists, and some as pastors and teachers, for the equipping of the saints for the work of service, to the building up of the body of Christ; until we all attain to the unity of the faith, and of the knowledge of the Son of God, to a mature man, to the measure of the stature which belongs to the fullness of Christ. As a result, we are no longer to be children, tossed here and there by waves and carried about by every wind of doctrine, by the trickery of men, by craftiness in deceitful scheming.[65]

For some reason, there seems to be an allergic reaction to learning from great Christians of antiquity, even though God Himself has given them to His Church. There are a couple of reasons that I believe this is the case. One reason comes from the belief that the Church became entirely heretical during the Middle Ages; therefore, people conclude, there is nothing to really learn from that era. This is not true; God has always had His people in every generation.

A second reason that I believe there is an allergic reaction to learning from great Christians from the past is simply laziness. It takes work to study and learn, especially if something was written in an older form of English. The use of one of these excuses should be something to be ashamed of, however. Those who came before us are still a part of the body of Christ. The body of Christ is not birthed anew with each generation; it exists from the first Christian God ever saved until the last. God has given us great pastors and teachers from the past who wrote things down, by the providence of God, for us to be able to read today. If God has given us pastors and teachers

---

in the past who have made great efforts to combat heresies and we will not learn from them, what does that say about our confidence that God will empower the proclamation of His truth? If we do not believe God has given us good theologians who have written creeds and books to guide the Church, then why do we go to church at all?

Preachers, in a sense, are theologians. If we cannot trust either living or dead human beings, why would a preacher preach? Why would a teacher teach? Why would anyone try to explain Scripture or set out bylaws for local congregations? If we cannot trust and learn from faithful pastors and teachers of antiquity, can we not trust pastors and teachers today? They are, after all, preaching the same Word of God as their predecessors; and God's Word is timeless. It crosses every generation and is relevant to every people group and every era from the first advent of Christ till the second advent. In other words, we do not trust God if we cannot trust His faithful ministers, whom He has given us no matter what era we are looking at. Many of the creeds and confessions of faith contain the richest, most useful, and most helpful summaries of God's Word ever written outside of Scripture.

We all understand that creeds and confessions are not inspired by God and not equal to Scripture. But in many instances, these creeds and confessions faithfully represent God's Word. If we learn from sermons today, why would we not learn from creeds and confessions? If we do not learn from the way the early Church dealt with issues and heresies, we are doomed to repeat them. Yes, we examine all things said in the name of God with Scripture. Yes, we cannot be gullible and accept the teachings of absolutely anyone. But if there have been thousands of faithful, discerning, and diligent Christians who all agree that a minister of antiquity was faithful to the Word of God, then he probably was; and he can be trusted today. Of course, there are exceptions to that, but learning about those exceptions would require taking classes on church history, which many churches do not offer.

One of the areas of theological failure that leads us to repeat the past is a failure to understand monergism. Monergism, after all, is a view that has been taught and handed down from the apostle Paul to Augustine to the Reformers and is still held today. Church history is filled with a biblical, monergistic view of God working in our lives and in our world. If you fail to understand or fail to accept monergism, you are the hero of your own story. You will never be able to understand the law of God and the imputed righteousness of Christ. You will always, consciously or unconsciously, attempt to claw your way out of the judgment required by the Law of God by your own power.

The prefix *mono* means one. The word *ergism* refers to a theological belief that good works are necessary for salvation. When you place the prefix *mono* in front of the noun *ergism*, you describe the theology that One has accomplished the good works necessary for justification. That One is Christ. Monergism is the belief that salvation is accomplished by God alone. *Syn* is another prefix you can place in front of *ergism*. *Syn* means "together" or "having the same function." Synergism is the belief that we work alongside God to have salvation. Monergism is often rejected because people, by nature, believe that salvation is something that should be able to be earned.

That is the one thing that all false religions have in common: people believe that you must earn your salvation. I could write another entire book on monergism, but I want to focus on how this can help us understand God's law in a greater way. Monergism is also true when it comes to sanctification. Ephesians 2 helps us see monergism in justification as well as in sanctification: "For by grace you have been saved through faith; and that not of yourselves, it is the gift of God; not as a result of works, so that no one may boast. For we are His workmanship, created in Christ Jesus for good works, which God prepared beforehand so that we would walk in them."[66] What Paul is saying is that even our works are not something that we can take credit for.

Progressive sanctification has to do with what we do because what we do helps us to grow in our Christlikeness. We cannot boast even in the works that we do because God has prepared each one of them before we were ever born. God is always the Hero and always gets the credit. Progressive sanctification is monergistic in the sense that God the Father has prepared it before we were ever born; God the Holy Spirit directs us toward it by working in our lives; and God the Son is our Example. When we cooperate with God in a way that we believe to be synergistic, what we are really doing is walking in the providence of God that has been guiding us all along. Nevertheless, the responsibility of growing in holiness falls upon you, just as the responsibility of believing the gospel falls on you whether you ever believe or whether you refuse to believe. We understand that, though, don't we?

The responsibility is ours, but it is God Who is at work and propels us because He is sovereign and gets all the glory and all the credit for anything good, holy, or righteous that we ever do in this life. God created us and saved us for good works that were prepared by God Himself before the world was created. If you can get hold of this reality, if you can wrap your mind around this truth, you will understand that there is no good that you can do on your own. You will understand that we are not overcomers because we are empowered not to sin. You will understand that anything that you ever do that has any righteousness to it at all is only because of Christ's imputed righteousness and God's perfect plan for you to accomplish that righteous deed from before you were ever born.

When you get to heaven, will you be able to boast that you were wiser, smarter, or more obedient than any other person? Will you be able to take even a degree of credit for your salvation? Will you get a percentage of glory that only belongs to God? Will you brag that you have more rewards than those standing around you? Or will you fall at His feet, take off your crown, and cast it at His feet because He has accomplished all these things despite you? God will get all the glory. We need to preach justification and sanctification as though we understand that. God has done everything for us. God is doing anything good that we ever will do through us, according to His plans. We have no ability to be righteous outside of Him, even in our deeds. Any good deeds that we ever do in this life were prepared before we were born. We are empowered by the Holy Spirit to accomplish these good things. When we get to Heaven, all we will be able to boast in is Christ and His accomplishments in us and through us. He gets all the credit; He gets all the glory.

CHAPTER 6

GOD BUILDS HIS CHURCH

"I also say to you that you are Peter, and upon this rock I will build My church; and the gates of Hades will not overpower it."

Matthew 16:18

The topics that we covered in previous chapters were meant to lead up to a discussion about how various things may inadvertently affect the decisions we make in life and local church leadership. Those previous chapters were meant to lay the ground for this chapter. One of the things we have focused on is the seemingly elusive sin of pride. But pride isn't the only thing that can influence us; pressure to succeed can also influence us. This is true in life, and this is true in the Church. We need and want to feel like we are not only accomplishing our mission but also like we are building and expanding. Our idea of success is not to keep things the way they are but to improve. And that is not always a bad thing.

It is good to take pride in our work in the sense of wanting to do a good job. It is good to want to leave things better than you first found them. It is good to want to be good at the ministry and make changes in things that we see could use improvement. But sometimes, the lines get crossed. Sometimes, we forget Whose Church we are improving. Sometimes, we forget local and denominational church leadership is responsible for the very bride of Christ, and we forget that He is a jealous Groom. Pressure to succeed can easily begin to influence our actions and decisions. Pressure to succeed can easily roll over into pride. At that point, pride can begin to stalk us; and we become grazing, unsuspecting sheep that want things to be done our way. And so, we turn to outside sources to see what we are doing wrong and how to improve—sources from seemingly successful local churches and sources from secular business practices that have been renamed as church growth models.

The reality is that when we cater our church services to the masses and what they want, we are harming the Church rather than building it. We lose our influence in society, our effectiveness in the Church, and our authority to correct a ship that is set off course. Church experts tell us that if we want to reach the world, we should find out what the world wants. In contrast, the truth is that for the Church to get its mission from the world is to render the Church impotent in a mission given by God Himself. People don't want to admit that they have been influenced by the masses—entangled in the vices of man. Many do not recognize when they have sprung the trap of Satan. That is why we need to learn to examine all things by the instructions of God, including ourselves and our motives. This takes humility and the working of the Holy Spirit upon our hearts.

Emotionalism has once again flooded the pews and oozed out into the streets. "You have a name that you are alive, but you are dead."[67] Emotionalism is fun. It is exciting because it draws its strength from the flesh, but it does so in the name of the Holy Spirit. In reality, the Holy Spirit is grieved because He wants us to glorify Christ. When people become captive to emotionalism, the flesh becomes glorified because experience supersedes biblical truth. Experience is emphasized over Christ. "Oh, but you have taken things too far now," some would say, "for it is experience in the name of Christ." Many wicked things have been done in the name of Christ over the centuries, but using the Lord's name in vain to jar people emotionally should be found in this very category.

Many pastors and teachers who capitalize on this emotionalism do so by claiming that God said things He did not say, even prefacing such claims with the phrase, "Thus says the Lord." Such use of God's name and authority becomes even worse when it involves manipulating God's name for the sake of profit. Why are we drawn to emotionalism without Christ rather than moved to be emotional because of Christ? To be emotional about the work of Christ is only natural. Emotionalism is misplaced where there is no personal familiarity with Christ, wisdom given by Christ, and understanding of Who Christ is and what He did.

So-called revival draws the masses from all over the country and even from all over the world because people do not understand what revival is. The concept of revival is found in the Old Testament, but it isn't what most people make it out to be today. Michael Brown said, "I define revival as a season of unusual divine visitation."[68] Revival is seen today as God moving in a supernatural way to save the lost when, in reality, revival only applies to Christians. To revive something means "to restore to life or consciousness."[69] It means "to restore something that is already there." So the definition of revival would be "restoring a church that has moved from Christianity into apostasy back to true Christianity."

Second Chronicles 29 is an example of revival, when King Hezekiah rediscovered the truths of Scripture: "Then he said to them, 'Listen to me, O Levites. Consecrate yourselves now, and consecrate the house of the Lord, the God of your fathers, and carry the uncleanness out from the holy place.'"[70] The Jews had become heretical in their worship, and Hezekiah brought the people back to true worship of God. This is revival. Revival includes the rediscovery of biblical truth. It includes repentance because of understanding biblical truth, it includes forgiveness, and it includes Christ-centered worship.

---

68   Michael Brown, "Has Revival Broken Out in America?" February 13, 2023, *The Line of Fire with Michael Brown*, YouTube video, 2:34-2:37, https://www.youtube.com/watch?v=HzSg9RMthk8.
69   *Oxford English Dictionary* (iPhone application, 2023), s.v. "revive."
70   2 Chronicles 29:5

Someone who is lost, who has committed apostasy, or who is heretical would never feel comfortable in true revival because the gospel is front and center rather than emotion. Someone who is lost needs to experience regeneration, not revival. Revival has never and will never be a planned event. When you are asking for revival, you are admitting that your church has become heretical. Revival can never be confined to a geographical location because it is the reconditioning of the heart.

Second Chronicles 34 is another good example of revival.

> When they were bringing out the money which had been brought into the house of the Lord, Hilkiah the priest found the book of the law of the Lord given by Moses. . . .[71] Moreover, Shaphan the scribe told the king saying, "Hilkiah the priest gave me a book." And Shaphan read from it in the presence of the king.

> When the king heard the words of the law, he tore his clothes. Then the king commanded Hilkiah, Ahikam the son of Shaphan, Abdon the son of Micah, Shaphan the scribe, and Asaiah the king's servant, saying, "Go, inquire of the Lord for me and for those who are left in Israel and in Judah, concerning the words of the book which has been found; for great is the wrath of the Lord which is poured out on us because our fathers have not observed the word of the Lord, to do according to all that is written in this book."[72]

The Bible had been lost over the course of time and, upon its rediscovery, the leaders realized they were in big trouble because they had not kept the law of God. They had abandoned what God had commanded. I recommend reading 2 Chronicles 29, 2 Chronicles 34, and 2 Kings 23, which show how bad things were in Israel just prior to the rediscovery of God's Word. But the question is, what would revival look like today? It would look like this:

---

71   2 Chronicles 34:14
72   2 Chronicles 34:18-21

removing the false practices, the false doctrines, and the false theologies that have crept into the church today and getting back to doing things the way we are commanded to by God Himself. It would mean repudiating false beliefs and practices such as wokeness, alternative sexual identities, the social gospel, and seeker-driven doctrine. It would mean examining so-called Christian music and worship to be sure that what we are singing is biblical and focused on the appreciation, adoration, glorification, and work of Christ.

The Protestant Reformation was an example of revival. The First Great Awakening was another example of revival. False doctrines and practices had infiltrated the Church, and God used individuals to point these things out to the Church by showing what Scripture teaches. The word *reform* means to re-form that which was once formed and over time was deformed. That is what reformation is—getting back to what Scripture teaches because apostasy has entered the building. We need reformation today. We need revival today that gets back to what has been lost. But revival done in this manner is different from what most people think about when they think of revival in the Church today. It was because of revival during the Reformation that many people became regenerated. It was because truth was front and center and was preached clearly and boldly.

Today, the word *revival* essentially describes the idea of attempting to force a supernatural work of God through a tangible experience—trying to get Him to change the atmosphere of a particular place for the purpose of an emotional high. This idea seems to assume that God is not present or cannot act unless a group of people have collectively crossed a particular emotional threshold. That is not how God works, and we don't have to perform some kind of magic ritual to summon Him. Jesus clarified the truth when He said, "'Again I say to you, that if two of you agree on earth about anything that they may ask, it shall be done for them by My Father who is in heaven. For where two or three have gathered together in My name, I am there in their midst."[73] God is fully with even two or three believers who have gathered together in His name. We are not commanded to seek anything more than God, and God is there with us in churches that have gathered together all across the world on any given day. Are we attempting to build God's church by worldly methods, or are we attempting to just be faithful in teaching what God speaks to us directly through Scripture?

> And coming to Him as to a living stone which has been rejected by men, but is choice and precious in the sight of God, you also, as living stones, are being built up as a spiritual house for a holy priesthood, to offer up spiritual sacrifices acceptable to God through Jesus Christ. For this is contained in Scripture: "Behold, I lay in Zion a choice stone, a precious corner stone, And he who believes in Him will not be disappointed." This precious value, then, is for you who believe; but for those who disbelieve, "The stone which the builders rejected, This became the very corner stone," and, "A stone of stumbling and a rock of offense"; for they stumble because they are disobedient to the word, and to this doom they were also appointed.[74]

"Are you not entertained? Is this not why you are here?" This is not only one of the famous quotes from Maximus in the movie *Gladiator*, but it also seems to be the mantra of many local churches today. This mantra started as what seemed to be a good idea—the idea that we should attract the world to the Church; and when we get them there, we hit them with the gospel. I might add that this is a failed idea because to keep those outside the family of God in the Church, you must not only entertain but also elevate the thrill of the hunt.

My mind wants to get to the root of the importance of entertainment. Why do people want to be entertained in the first place? It seems our society lives for entertainment. Many people spend most of their hard-earned

---

73   Matthew 18:19-20
74   1 Peter 2:4-8

money on movies, games, toys, sports . . . the list goes on and on. But why? One of the reasons is because life is hard. It is difficult, and an escape from reality seems so soothing—an opportunity to sit and bask in a world in which I can turn off my mind and let the problems of today and tomorrow slip away for a little while. That is what movies and video games do for you. You can live the life of another—the life you wish you had. You can live a life of purpose, meaning, romance, or adventure. Other people want to actually use their minds but in a different way—to focus on solving a problem that has nothing to do with their problem. So we have puzzles and other thinking challenges, but they still do the same thing for us, don't they? They are an escape from the problems and consequences we face in day-to-day life. There are some people who satisfy their sexual desires with entertainment. We are driven; we long; and we can be eccentric in our quest to be entertained because entertainment is a source of purpose, escape, or happiness for a season. But what are the implications of this quest? It really has to do with satisfaction, doesn't it? We are, after all, dealing with the way the Church is built and by whom—by us or by God.

Why do some local churches believe that the Church should be an expositor of entertainment rather than an expositor of God's Word? It is because we have bought into the devil's lies. When the Church's focus is on entertainment rather than Christ, the Church has turned to the wisdom of Satan. He wants the Church's focus to be on anything but Christ; and if he can tempt us with "the lust of the flesh," "the lust of the eyes," or "the pride of life,"[75] he has won. Some local churches believe their purpose is to build God's Church rather than rest in His sovereign plan. Does God's Church need a gimmick? Does God's Church need to be attractive to the world? The answer is no.

Don't get me wrong—there is wholesome and good entertainment. I personally like to be entertained, but that is not what I want when I go

---

75   1 John 2:16

to church. To be honest, the Church is really bad at entertainment in the first place—maybe because it was never intended to be good at such. I find it nauseating when a pastor or some other leader gets in front of the congregation and cracks jokes. I find it sickening when music in the church is directed toward the elevation of man rather than the admiration and worship of God Himself. Whatever happened to being sober-minded? Whatever happened to the awe of being with fellow Christians in an assembly dedicated to glorifying our Lord and Savior who died to save us from the wrath of God? Whatever happened to the anguish over sin and the joy over redemption? Why aren't we crushed? Because we are entertained. Why aren't we in awe over God's mercy poured out on wicked sinners? Because we are entertained. We are entertained because we believe the ignorant and bombastic idea that we build God's Church.

When church services are done in line with the ways of people and in a way that is meant to be pleasing to the lost, it has a counterintuitive effect. We lose our influence in society because the Church should be countercultural. We cannot influence the people in the world when we are like them. So when they come to the Church and into the church building for hope, for peace, and for answers, only to find we are no different than the help they can find in secular programs, we have failed to be faithful in our mission. Jesus said:

> "You are the salt of the earth; but if the salt has become tasteless, how can it be made salty again? It is no longer good for anything, except to be thrown out and trampled under foot by men. "You are the light of the world. A city set on a hill cannot be hidden; nor does anyone light a lamp and put it under a basket, but on the lampstand, and it gives light to all who are in the house. Let your light shine before men in such a way that they may see your good works, and glorify your Father who is in heaven.[76]

The Word of God is relevant in every era—to every culture and ethnicity. To think we can improve it to make it more relatable or change it to be relevant to the times or the culture is to think ourselves to be wiser than God Himself. Again, this is something that we must realize because we tend to stay in the rut we have carved out until that rut is pointed out by a book written to point out such ruts (like this one), a discerning pastor or member of a local church, or the Word of God.

God builds His Church. The reality is that He doesn't need us. Luke writes, "The God who made the world and all things in it, since He is Lord of heaven and earth, does not dwell in temples made with hands; nor is He served by human hands, as though He needed anything, since He Himself gives to all people life and breath and all things."[77] All these negative influences that we have been talking about in this study all boil down to the rejection of this fact, and everything positive that we have discussed boils down to the acceptance of this fact: He doesn't need us. That should humble us.

I think of my children when they were young. I didn't need them to work on a car, to frame a wall, or to build a fence. In fact, getting them involved made any project I was working on much more difficult. It took longer, I had to worry about their safety; and I had to instruct and direct them. So why do we get our children involved in things that we are doing? Because we love them. God doesn't need us, but He loves us. He wants us to get involved in His work—that is His design—and that is a great privilege. We are toddlers with hammers and saws. We are infants who sometimes think we know better than our Father. And He is just that—our Father. The truth that that fact alone does not strike us and render us shaking in our boots shows that we do not know Him like we should.

God builds His Church. The gates of Hades (that is, the power of death) will not stop Him, and neither will people. He is omnipotent and sovereign, and He has given us instruction on what we can and cannot do. During the

---

77 Acts 17:24-25

time of the Protestant Reformation two views emerged concerning worship: the regulative principle and the normative principle. The regulative principle is the view that God has given us boundaries in Scripture regarding how to worship Him that we cannot violate. The normative principle is the view that God has given us freedom to worship Him in any way that is not forbidden in Scripture. Most congregations today hold to the normative principle, even though they may not understand what that means. Nadab and Abihu also believed in the normative principle of worship: "Now Nadab and Abihu, the sons of Aaron, took their respective firepans, and after putting fire in them, placed incense on it and offered strange fire before the Lord, which He had not commanded them. And fire came out from the presence of the Lord and consumed them, and they died before the Lord."[78]

We are not playing games with God. We don't have the freedom to go outside or above what He commands. We are to be faithful in what He has given us and what He has instructed us to do. It is a very serious thing to be in church leadership. We cannot take the Bride of Christ lightly. God will build His church and bury us underneath her if we do not approach His Bride with humility.

CHAPTER 7
SUBMISSION AND HUMILITY

"FOR GOD IS OPPOSED TO THE PROUD,
BUT GIVES GRACE TO THE HUMBLE."

1 Peter 5:5b

Friedrich Nietzsche was a German philosopher who is famous for declaring the death of God: "Thus, the devil once spoke to me: 'Even God has his hell: it is his love for mankind.' And recently, I heard him say these words: 'God is dead: God died of his pity for mankind.'"[79]

Nietzsche believed that Christianity was responsible for weakness in culture, and he believed that weakness in culture was the cause of civil decline. He seemed to be conflicted in many ways because he understood that Christian values were what held society together, yet he also blamed Christianity for softening society because of its values. He believed that Christianity blocked a person off from the true meaning of life, which was found by the empowerment of self. And because of that, strength had been lost; and only weakness remained. An authentic person, he believed, was a conqueror. Authentic people didn't cave in to weakness, meekness, or humility. He called this conqueror an *Übermensch*, which means "superman."

---

79   Friedrich Nietzsche, "On the Pitying," in *Thus Spake Zarathustra* (New York City: Simon & Brown, 2018), 41.

Did Nietzsche bring a new idea to philosophy, or did he only verbalize what has been written on the heart of man since the fall of man? The natural man, after all, hates humility, hates submission to authority, and really has no idea what these things actually mean. Humility doesn't mean weakness of character. Submission doesn't mean mindless following. The Christian faith isn't blind faith, and the Christian religion isn't for the cowardly. Nietzsche only declared what the cry of the world is—a world that is lost in a darkened room.

In some ways Nietzsche was right. His point really wasn't that God died— he didn't believe in God in the first place—his point was that Christianity, as a worldview, had diminished in influence because of the Age of Enlightenment. His point was that there was no need for religion anymore because of scientific breakthroughs. He was correct that the Enlightenment changed the dominant worldview from one based on the Bible (which was supported by reason and science) to one based on reason and science alone, which excluded the Bible. He was correct that the Church had lost its influence.

The idea of atheism brings hopelessness; and within that train of thought "God [or religion] has his [its] hell: his [its] love for mankind." There is no room for love for people if there is no God. Atheism is the pinnacle of prideful self-centeredness because you must get all you can out of this life, and then you die. Nietzsche was correct, if you hold to atheism, that "God" or religion "is dead: God [or religion] died of his [its] pity for mankind." If life is all about you, the only purpose for life is something external and transient. That is what pride does in the hearts of people—it leaves no pity for other people. If religion is dead—no longer needed—then humility is to be despised, and life is all about being a superman. But Scripture has a different view of mankind. It brings true purpose to life. It starts with showing us that life isn't all about us. That is where humility comes into play. Scripture really tears us down first so that we can be made strong in God.

Scripture is full of slave language. We don't like that—even Bible translators fear this stigma because of the history of slavery in nineteenth-century

Europe and America and because Christians in the West live in societies that prize freedom. We understand the heinous things that are associated with slavery. We understand the terrible things that were done to our fellow human beings. So it is understandable that Bible translators have tried to steer away from using this word when dealing with biblical texts. They fear translating the Greek word *doulos* as "slave" in most cases. Instead, they translate it as "servant" or "bondservant." *Doulos* only means "slave"—they are aware of that—but that carries with it a lot of baggage. But when understood rightly, it is a very beautiful thing.

The word "Lord" is the Greek word *Kurios*. A *kurios* always has a *doulos*. That is what we are—we are literally slaves to God. There are two different reactions to this news: pride or humility. What is your reaction? A good question to ask to help figure that out is this: what is your view of God? Answering that question will, in turn, help to calm the emotions that result from realizing you are a slave. Is God a good God, or is He a cruel God? A cruel God would not give mercy. A cruel God would not love His elect unconditionally. A cruel God wouldn't die for you, and a cruel God would never give you amazing grace.

What does it mean that "God gives grace to the humble"? It means that we are all flawed and desperately need God's grace. Grace means receiving something that you do not deserve. We do not deserve God's grace—that alone is humbling. God isn't obligated to give us grace. He doesn't bestow upon us grace out of a response to obedience. That would be the opposite of grace. That would be a wage or getting what we earned or deserve. Never ask God to give you what you deserve. All that we deserve is His wrath. What we should ask God for His mercy and grace. God gives grace to those who understand it is undeserved.

Christianity is the very essence of humility. Look at our Savior, Who is our prime example. He humbly took on the nature of man to save us and give us hope and a future beyond what we can ever imagine. He humbly walked among us. He humbly allowed His creation to lie about Him to see Him murdered. He humbly allowed His persecutors to pull out His beard, thrust a crown of thorns onto His head, strip Him naked, beat Him within inches of His life, and ultimately nail Him to a cross. He gave His persecutors the strength to do that. He expanded their lungs as their breath increased because of their labor while beating Him. He allowed their heartbeats to intensify under the labor of nailing Him to a cross. He allowed their blood to flow into their fingertips as they crafted the crown of thorns. He is our ultimate example of humility. And this is amazing because God isn't dependent, weak, and mortal. But out of His grace, He shares some of His attributes with you and with me. When you were hopeless, He died for you. You are hopeless without Him, but He made a way for you to have hope.

"Therefore humble yourselves under the mighty hand of God, that He may exalt you at the proper time."[80] If you see God, this is a natural response. If you know Him, you will fall at His feet in worship. The way we see Him and know Him is through His Word. Scripture is about Him. Scripture is about Jesus. Scripture is not about you. You don't read it to know how to be a better Law-abiding citizen; you read it to know Him better, and that is what changes you. "Humble yourselves under the mighty hand of God." And for what reason? "That He may exalt you at the proper time." You don't exalt yourself. God exalts those who are humble. God exalts those who know their real identity as weak, dependent, and needy people who rely on Him for their very breath. God will exalt those who know Him; do you know Him? Do you spend time using not only your heart but also your mind reading, studying, and striving to know Him?

Nietzsche taught that the individual should conquer without the help of a make-believe god that was crippling society. His view called for an inner strength, charisma, and self-reliance. That is impossible, but it also brings to light another problem: where do strength, charisma, and self-reliance

---

come from? Early Greek scholars realized something that Nietzsche either didn't understand or that Nietzsche rejected. They understood that for something to be, or to exist, there must be a being that has always existed from which all other things that exist derive their existence. They called this entity the *Logos*. Plato made a distinction between the *Logos* and things that derive their existence from the *Logos*. He called the *Logos* "being" and called creatures "becomings."

There must be a being that does not rely upon anything to sustain it or there could be no becoming. John borrowed from that and wrote: "In the beginning was the Word [*Logos*], and the Word [*Logos*] was with God, and the Word [*Logos*] was God. He was in the beginning with God. All things came into being through Him, and apart from Him nothing came into being that has come into being."[81] The fundamental flaw of Nietzsche's philosophy is that people cannot be the source of their own power but must rely on and depend on something or someone else. The *Logos* depends on nothing; we call this aseity. The *Logos* had no beginning and will have no ending. The *Logos* is God; and it is by means of Him and through Him that we have life. It is by means of Him and through Him that we have resources to sustain us. We are dependent on God for everything; it is in Him we have life. It is in Him that we can "move and exist" (Acts 17:28). Humility must be our response to our recognition of this fact. We do not conquer using inside sources—there are no inside sources—we conquer using God's sources. There is no such thing as self-reliance; there is only dependence on the *Logos* from Whom all power and ability comes.

The Christian is a conqueror, but not from within; we are conquering through Christ. There are no "lone wolf" Christians. We have no ability to conquer anything; we are purchased and placed into Christ, Who is the Conqueror. We can only overcome anything at all because we are in Him. The word *humble* or *humility* is used approximately eighty-eight times in Scripture for a reason. Humility is bowing before the throne of God and recognizing

81 John 1:1-3

that you are nothing without Him. Humility is clinging to Him in the face of difficulty, rather than going it alone or with the power of some outside source. Humility is understanding that we live in total darkness—that we are lost and damned until the light of the gospel is proclaimed and God changes our hearts. Humility is admitting that the only reason you can do good things in life is because God has set those good things in front of you before you were born for you to achieve them. It is humbling to understand that God chose you—not because of what you have done, a decision you made, or because you are smarter and greater than your neighbor but because of His good and perfect pleasure.

The world tells you that you are wonderful, deserve great things, and are special. But what happens when people are told by everyone around them that they are awesome, amazing, priceless, and deserve to get the things they desire out of life? Either self-righteousness or disappointment is what happens. You either buy into the illusion that what they say about you is true and ignore the haters because they don't know you; or you become a failure when you realize that you are not all those wonderful things that people say you are, and self-disappointment sets in, which leads to depression. That is the wisdom of the world.

Humility is something that we can never fully achieve. We never arrive at humility as though it is some destination. In fact, humility is not something that we can ever really see in ourselves; it is seen by others. The reason for this is that as soon as you believe you are humble, you have just been filled with humility's antithetical counterpart—pride. Humility doesn't mean weakness of character. Humility doesn't mean silence; it doesn't mean going along with the flow; it doesn't mean never voicing disagreement. Jesus is our primary Example of humility; yet He fashioned a whip, flipped over tables, and drove people out of His Father's house when He saw that it had been corrupted. It takes a great deal of humility to rebuke, to correct, or to exhort someone even when that rebuke, correction, or exhortation is done in and through the working of the Holy Spirit rather than personal pride. We must set aside what people think of us if we truly want to help them see their sin and disobedience clearly.

It is very difficult to go to a brother or sister in Christ and rebuke that person out of love rather than anger. Humility is very different from what most people in the Church today believe it is. Humility is realizing when someone offends you, "But if not for God, I would be worse." Humility must be pursued, even though we must also understand that it can never be overtaken. We need to stop seeing humility as though it is something isolated from or outside of the other communicable attributes of God. Humility must be reconciled with all the other characteristics of the Christian life. Sometimes, people use humility as a weapon to rebuke others by saying that those others weren't humble in the way they went about doing something. Yet that isn't always the case because strength, truth, and boldness are connected to humility. That connection exists because all these qualities radiate from God.

I think of King Nebuchadnezzar when the topic of humility comes up:

> The king reflected and said, "Is this not Babylon the great, which I myself have built as a royal residence by the might of my power and for the glory of my majesty?" While the word was in the king's mouth, a voice came from heaven, saying, "King Nebuchadnezzar, to you it is declared: sovereignty has been removed from you, and you will be driven away from mankind, and your dwelling place will be with the beasts of the field. You will be given grass to eat like cattle, and seven periods of time will pass over you until you recognize that the Most High is ruler over the realm of mankind and bestows it on whomever He wishes." Immediately the word concerning Nebuchadnezzar was fulfilled; and he was driven away from mankind and began eating grass like cattle, and his body was drenched with the dew of heaven until his hair had grown like eagles' feathers and his nails like birds' claws.

"But at the end of that period, I, Nebuchadnezzar, raised my eyes toward heaven and my reason returned to me, and I blessed the Most High and praised and honored Him who lives forever; For His dominion is an everlasting dominion, And His kingdom endures from generation to generation. "All the inhabitants of the earth are accounted as nothing, But He does according to His will in the host of heaven And among the inhabitants of earth; And no one can ward off His hand Or say to Him, 'What have You done?' At that time my reason returned to me. And my majesty and splendor were restored to me for the glory of my kingdom, and my counselors and my nobles began seeking me out; so I was reestablished in my sovereignty, and surpassing greatness was added to me. Now I, Nebuchadnezzar, praise, exalt and honor the King of heaven, for all His works are true and His ways just, and He is able to humble those who walk in pride."[82]

King Nebuchadnezzar learned humility the hard way so that we could read his story and learn. We must see ourselves as Nebuchadnezzar rather than pointing the finger and crying "idiot."

The other biblical doctrine that Nietzsche despised was submission. Jesus is also our example of submission. Something that many people do not think about is what a sacrifice it was for Christ to take on the nature of man and, in so doing, to be fully submissive to the Father. Jesus is perfectly united within the Trinity. In other words, there has never been any disagreement within the Trinity; there has never been anything missing or lacking within the Trinity; and there never will be any disagreement or lack. There is only perfect unity in every aspect of all things within the Trinity because that is what perfection looks like, and God is perfect in all things. For Him to take on the nature of man, being truly Man (as the Chalcedonian Creed so rightly teaches), means that He took on that nature everlastingly. To be truly man, you must have both soul and body. Jesus was born truly man with both soul and body, exactly as we are, yet without the sin nature because He was born of the virgin Mary and because of the activity of the Holy Spirit in His conception. That act alone (taking on the nature of man) is astounding. He began His life as a man being submissive to the perfect plan of God that was established before the creation of the universe.

Another time Jesus was submissive to God was at His baptism. John was baptizing people for the purpose of repentance. Jesus didn't need to repent or be forgiven because Jesus is sinless. He was baptized to "fulfill all righteousness."[83] Jesus said in John 6, "'For I have come down from heaven, not to do My own will, but the will of Him who sent Me.'"[84]

The time that all Christians ought to think about when dealing with the submissiveness of Christ to the Father is in the Garden of Gethsemane. If you remember, as Jesus was praying, He said these words: "'My Father, if it is possible, let this cup pass from Me; yet not as I will, but as You will.'"[85] Jesus was about to face the most difficult event in history—the imputation of our sin to Himself. He would pay for our sin at the cross; and because of His submission, we would have eternal life.

I must say here that Christ being submissive to the Father doesn't mean that Jesus did anything that He did not want to do: "For this reason the Father loves Me, because I lay down My life so that I may take it again. No one has taken it away from Me, but I lay it down on My own initiative. I have authority to lay it down, and I have authority to take it up again. This commandment I received from My Father.'"[86] "No one" takes anything away from Christ, let alone His "life"; He laid "it down on His own initiative." Jesus was not only submissive but also wanted to die for His elect.

Submission doesn't mean mindless following. It doesn't mean blind faith. Our faith is to be a very cognitive faith with a foundation that becomes

---

83   Matthew 3:15
84   John 6:38
85   Matthew 26:39
86   John 10:17-18

strong and real as we are transformed by the renewing of our minds. We follow because we are called to follow and supplied with the knowledge that is necessary for us to understand why we follow. We submit to the authority of God because we know Who He is and what He has done. Submission, to a Christian, isn't a burden but an honor. Submission has two things behind it: fear and love.

Proverbs is the book most people think about when the subject of the fear of God comes to mind. "The fear of the LORD is the beginning of knowledge." "The fear of the LORD is the beginning of wisdom." "The fear of the LORD is to hate evil." "The fear of the LORD prolongs life." "He who walks in his uprightness fears the LORD." "The fear of the LORD is a fountain of life." "How blessed is the man who fears always."[87]

To fear God is to submit to His authority, but there is more to it than that. There is an idea of the fear of God that is too strong, and there is an idea of the fear of God that is too weak. To fear God because He is unloving and wishes to harm us every time that we mess up is a wrong view. To say that what the Bible means by fearing God is really to respect Him is also a wrong view. You will not have the proper kind of fear of God if you do not know Him. You get to know Him through a good study of theology, focusing generally on theology proper and specifically on the attributes of God. When you begin to know God, you will fear Him because He is magnified to His proper place in your mind. The reality of His awesomeness and infinite glory becomes not only something you have heard but also something you know in a greater way. To fear God is more than respect, and it is less than being terrified—it is to know Him. It is something that cannot be put into words; it is something that you understand because a formerly distorted view of God becomes more accurate and clearer. This is when submission becomes no longer a task but a natural way of life. This is when the reason you submit is no longer just obedience but also love.

---

87 Proverbs 1:7; 9:10; 8:13; 10:27; 14:2; 14:27; 28:14

We submit to God because we love Him. This isn't something surface. This isn't something superficial. It isn't something found in the world. This is a Godlike love that can only be experienced by His own. I am talking about something that cannot be written down; this reality is something that, even if the greatest orator of our time wrote it down, would seem too cheap to those who experience this kind of love. I am not talking about emotionalism or some kind of euphoric experience that is found in Hinduism and many Charismatic churches. I am talking about a response to a realization that happens in a person's mind. That is my desire in writing this book—to motivate you to pursue something tangible that is not found in a shallow pond. It is not found on the surface of the ocean. It is found by deep, hard, and intentional study.

And even in this, we find a knife's edge because some people want greater knowledge for the purpose of being puffed up. But knowledge, for the sake of intellectual dominance, is antithetical to love. When you study theology proper, it should humble you. If you are going in the opposite direction, there should be flashing red lights all around you warning and screaming that you are diving headlong into pride—the very quagmire of the devil. Love isn't something I can command you to learn. Love isn't some feeling or temporary emotional response to God's work in your life. Love is an earnest and steadfast commitment that involves an occasional emotional response. Love is seeking the face of God and learning everything that there is to know about Him; and when you find that path, submission becomes a way of life.

CHAPTER 8
DEPENDENCE

"De-pend-ence: The state of relying on or being controlled by someone or something else."[88]

The dependency theory is a school of thought in social science that aims to comprehend underdevelopment within an ethnic or social group. Its goal is to identify the origins of dependence on governmental leadership to combat Marxist ideologies. In many instances, those ideas are believed to originate in Western countries and imposed on developing countries to keep them from developing. The idea is that if you are in a state of dependence, you will never overcome the controlling forces that keep you from excelling.

The idea of dependence illustrates the difference between wisdom that is from the world and wisdom that is a gift of God. It is true that we do not want to be dependent on the government, a program, a person, or anything else. It is true that one part of growing from a baby to an adult is learning independence and self-reliance. But when it comes to God and His kingdom, we need to learn that the same way of thinking cannot and must not be applied. We are dealing with a different kind of wisdom—one that has a much greater purpose. We are dealing with something eternal—something infinitely beyond ourselves.

---

88   *Oxford English Dictionary* (iPhone application, 2023), s.v. "dependence."

In the world, dependence can be a bad thing. There are some people that are codependent on other people. Some are dependent on narcotics, alcohol, or other substances. Dependence is looked at as something bad or something broken. The colonies that became the United States didn't want to be dependent upon Great Britain; the colonists wanted their independence (an independence that continues to this day), and they fought and earned it through much bloodshed and sacrifice. Christian dependence is very different from that. Christian dependence doesn't mean we are pushovers prone to being bullied—just the opposite. It means that we draw on a source of strength that is outside of ourselves. We may be part of a collective; but the collective has a Head, and that Head is Christ. To be in Him and fully dependent on Him is a great joy.

We are a collective body of Christ. A collective has a singular goal—a mission—and that mission, for a child of the King, is to glorify Him. We should see our mission and purpose as something greater than ourselves. We are a part of something that goes beyond and outside of time and space—we are a part of the Ancient of Days. We are not part of Him in a Gnostic way—we are not divine—but as the body of Christ: "Since there is one bread, we who are many are one body; for we all partake of the one bread."[89]

Paul said again in 1 Corinthians, "For even as the body is one and yet has many members, and all the members of the body, though they are many, are one body, so also is Christ. For by one Spirit we were all baptized into one body, whether Jews or Greeks, whether slaves or free, and we were all made to drink of one Spirit."[90] If we take the time to really understand this, we see that it means that we are dependent creatures. "We were all made to drink of one Spirit" communicates a picture of a source of life that we should thirst for—a thirst that cannot be quenched from any other source outside of the workings of God—and that we each collectively drink from the same source. We become malnourished when we deprive ourselves of this intimate dependence on God.

Not only are we dependent upon God, but we are also dependent upon one another within the body of Christ.

> For the body is not one member, but many. If the foot says, "Because I am not a hand, I am not a part of the body," it is not for this reason any the less a part of the body. And if the ear says, "Because I am not an eye, I am not a part of the body," it is not for this reason any the less a part of the body. If the whole body were an eye, where would the hearing be? If the whole were hearing, where would the sense of smell be? But now God has placed the members, each one of them, in the body, just as He desired. If they were all one member, where would the body be?[91]

Dependence is the way of life for the Christian. We depend on God, and we depend on one another; that is His design. Sometimes in the Church, we have people who want to be mouths when they are hands. Sometimes in the Church, we have people who are eyes in the body of Christ but want to be noses. We should understand that this mismatch would be something other than what God created those people to be. Each person in the body of Christ has been given a gift for ministry, and it is the task of that individual to understand what that gift is. We have elders that can help us with that also, but it is important not to be plugged into the wrong ministry.

Because the Church is created to be characterized by interdependence, it often suffers because its members become dormant. It is an easy thing for local church leaders to just want to fill slots that need to be filled without looking closely—without taking the time to see if they are plugging an ear into the slot of a foot. Mistakes are okay; but when you realize, either as part of the leadership or as an individual, that you may have been placed into the wrong slot, then to not resolve that problem is to fail as a church member. You should pursue a resolution to that problem with great prayer, seeking the will of God about where you should serve. For some people, finding what their gift is could be a difficult task. Sometimes, people get plugged into many slots until they understand what they are called to do, and that is okay.

The worst examples I have seen of this misplacement within a biblical congregation occur in the music ministry. Many people want to be on stage. They may like to sing, and they may like to play; but sometimes, they simply are not skilled. It is an act of harm and borderline abuse when leadership recognizes this yet fails to remove those people from the music ministry. What happens in this situation is that the members that are plugged into the wrong slot never develop the skills for what God has called them to do because they are already serving. They become complacent. You may have teachers who never become teachers because they are on stage. You may have people gifted in administration who are too busy with the music ministry that they are obviously not gifted in, so they never truly learn to serve where they are gifted.

This is true in so many kinds of ministries. We fail in leadership or as individuals when we realize that we are eyes who enjoy being tongues but never change. I really wish I could sing. I would love to be on the stage of the church leading with an amazing voice, but the truth is that I cannot sing. If local church leaders were afraid that I would leave a particular local church if they told me no, that would be the opposite of what I need. To intentionally or lackadaisically continue in a ministry you are not called to do is to never learn dependence. You are forcing something. You are being something you were never called to be. That isn't dependence. That is pride.

Speaking of praise and worship, do you understand that one of the things we are doing when we worship God through song is crying out that we are dependent? We are saying, "God, we need You; we depend on You; we understand this, so we sing to You." One of the things I use to evaluate if I will sing a song at church is the question, "Who is this song pointing to as being the object of my praise?" So many songs that are sung in the church today are pointing to the individual, to Heaven, or to some benefit of being a follower of Christ; but that isn't worship. We should be made small by worship, and God should made great by worship. The object of our worship should be Christ. We should have theologically rich lyrics that magnify God. The more we magnify God, the more we become desperate because we begin to understand that we are nothing without Him. We are totally dependent upon God for everything in life. Worship Him in a way that shows you depend on Him, and you will begin to mature as a believer.

We are to be dependent on one another, and we are dependent (and we are to continue to be dependent) on God. To be successful at that dependence is to serve one another and to serve God with the gifts that He Himself has given you.

> On the contrary, it is much truer that the members of the body which seem to be weaker are necessary; and those members of the body which we deem less honorable, on these we bestow more abundant honor, and our less presentable members become much more presentable, whereas our more presentable members have no need of it. But God has so composed the body, giving more abundant honor to that member which lacked, so that there may be no division in the body, but that the members may have the same care for one another. And if one member suffers, all the members suffer with it; if one member is honored, all the members rejoice with it.[92]

There is what seems like a fine line between dependence and sanctification. Many churches teach a synergistic view of sanctification. Perhaps they do that inadvertently, or perhaps they are prone to legalism.

The Christian is pulled in one of two wrong directions—either legalism or antinomianism. Churches have become heretical by falling off one of these two cliffs. Legalism is adding rules that go above and beyond what is found in Scripture and deeming those rules to be a necessity whether in redemption or sanctification. Antinomianism literally means "no law" and is the idea that the law of God is no longer for us today. Both views are wrong. We really learn how sanctification works in a greater way when we place it within the category of dependence. In other words, we can do nothing for God without the working of the Holy Spirit working our salvation out of us.

"So then, my beloved, just as you have always obeyed, not as in my presence only, but now much more in my absence, work out your salvation with fear and trembling; for it is God who is at work in you, both to will and to work for His good pleasure."[93] We "work out our salvation." That means that we literally "work out" what is inside of us. Who has placed anything good inside of us? God. The indwelling Holy Spirit has objectives planned for our lives for us to accomplish. Those things are "worked out" in the Christian life. The reason we "work out our salvation"—or good deeds because of salvation—"with fear and trembling" is to teach us that we are dependent upon God. Let me put it another way: what would be worked out of us if we had no fear of God? The answer is a work that would be independent of His power, which would have no goodness to it at all.

There really isn't a fine line between dependence and sanctification. We don't always realize that there is no line between dependence and sanctification because the Holy Spirit is working in the background to change our desires, responses, and reactions and to help us to be obedient to God's commandments. I think we would all agree that obedience would never be something we can accomplish on our own apart from the Holy

---

Spirit. That is the purpose of the law altogether: to show us our reliance on God both in justification and in progressive sanctification. The difference between a believer and a nonbeliever is just that: the Holy Spirit who indwells us and propels us to grow in Christlikeness. Though the Holy Spirit is busy at work in us, it is possible for us to reject His guidance. In fact, it is more than possible; it is probable, as we all know because we need to repent daily. That is what happens when we stop being dependent and start wanting to do things our own way. That is why Philippians 2:12 is a commandment. What we should realize here is that we do not bring out the work of the Holy Spirit through our actions; but rather, the Holy Spirit drives our actions toward a greater holiness that God has planned from the very beginning.

God will guarantee that good works are accomplished with or without you. In other words, He doesn't need us. God didn't create us because He was lonely. God doesn't use us because He is incapable. God doesn't need our good works to make Him feel fulfilled or accomplished. God is perfectly united within the Trinity (the Father, the Son, and the Holy Spirit fully agree on everything they decide) and is fully self-sufficient. We should be humbled that He uses us to do anything. Sometimes, we get this idea that God would not accomplish a mission, such as salvation or good works to a neighbor or stranger, without us. But God will accomplish His purposes with or without you. When you refuse to submit to His calling, someone else will be called. Someone else will receive the blessing of doing what you have failed to do for Him.

The reason we miss out or refuse to submit can often be because we lack confidence, boldness, or kindness. It can also be because we lack a sense of urgency. Two of these things are found in understanding, and walking in, dependence. Both a lack of confidence and a lack of boldness come from believing that you accomplish things by your own will, determination, and power (and on your own timetable). Most people would never admit that;

but we want to get to the root of an issue, and that is the root. We do not want to miss the blessing of God because we have a lack of understanding of Whose strength we rely on to accomplish these good works we have been called to do. We should move forward with total confidence and with total boldness because we understand that we are called by God Himself to accomplish a given task for His kingdom. We should also move forward with total confidence and with total boldness because we understand that we are doing this by means of His power and His call. We don't depend on our own strength and ability. We don't depend on motivation from outside sources. We should learn to depend fully and totally on God; and when we learn and live this out, there will be nothing that He has called us to do that will be too great to be accomplished.

CHAPTER 9
IN WEAKNESS

"And He has said to me, 'My grace is sufficient for you, for power is perfected in weakness.' Most gladly, therefore, I will rather boast about my weaknesses, so that the power of Christ may dwell in me."

2 Corinthians 12:9

Because I have a type A personality, I used to think weakness was something that needed to be squeezed out of me. It was something I didn't like about myself, and it was something I took no pity on when I spotted it in other people. Looking back, I recognize that I needed to learn two things: how to love and how to be weak.

I joined the police department when I was younger with the goal of being a S.W.A.T. officer in the front of my mind. I accomplished my goal. Success was something I was familiar with, since I had been highly driven most of my life. I worked hard and was placed on the S.W.A.T. team after only two years of service. I loved it, and I loved the idea of being a S.W.A.T. officer. What I didn't anticipate was how being in this position would cause me to wrestle with my Christianity—a very immature Christianity, at that.

We went through a lot of training, and one of the most fundamental objectives was learning how to control our minds—our thoughts—if, and when, we were forced into a situation in which we had to squeeze the trigger on a threat. We were really taught to remove the human element from the situation—to locate and stop a threat by either communication or by violence of action. The reality is that a threat is more than a threat; a threat is a person. If you are a S.W.A.T. officer and you find yourself in this type of situation, you have no time to think because the seconds you take to think through a situation give threats the time to remove *their* threat—you. So we were trained in how to desensitize ourselves. We were trained in how to take a life and not think about it—to be smoothly running unstoppable machines.

I understand that. I understand why people struggle with these issues because I have been there, because I have trained, and because I have been in real-life situations. No one wants to take a human life; but if you are a S.W.A.T. officer, you must be ready and willing before the moment comes if you are going to survive and accomplish the mission. Most missions were to save a life in the first place. You had to be ready. Both your body and your mind had to be ready, sharp, and focused. Not only is your life at risk but also those of your team members are at risk. They depend on you because they train with you. Their lives are also at risk, and failure at your job could cost other people their lives.

Because I was exposed to these things, I began to wrestle with a tension between my Christianity and my training. I found myself calloused and without emotion, in a very dark place. I began to embrace it. I began to take pride in the husk of a man I had become. It is easier to be empty than to feel. That is when God, through His love and providence, showed me what I was becoming. I began to ask myself, "But how do I find balance? How do I find peace with both my God and my mission?" I turned to Scripture, which is the correct thing to do in any situation. I began to read about David. David was a warrior and a man after God's own heart. He became my influence and my hero in many ways. Yet I was focused on the wrong things in the life of David. I was focused on his capability and strength, but I failed to realize what the Source of David's strength and capability was. I focused on the wrong things because I hated weakness. It was an enemy.

I am not talking about weakness of mind or weakness in character. I am not talking about physical weakness or inability—not entirely, anyway. I am really talking about recognizing the source of our abilities. If we have any ability to think and reason, what is the source of that ability? If we have any character at all, where does that come from? If we have any physical ability to do anything at all, even to blink our eyelids, from where does that strength come? All these qualities play a part in what I am talking about; but ultimately, I am talking about weakness in spirit, or, as Jesus said, "'Blessed are the poor in spirit.'"[94]

Weakness is really what this book is about—learning what Paul means when he says that God's power is perfected in weakness. I believe this is one of the most misunderstood realities in the Church today. We are taught to be strong and courageous by clinging to the truths of Scripture, yet the emphasis is often upon our ability to apply the sermon and the Bible to our lives. This is a half-truth. Scripture never makes the claim that we are to be strong and courageous by gritting our teeth. It never teaches that we can do anything at all by our own strength. It doesn't even teach that God gives us strength and courage through greater obedience to His law. Scripture teaches that we are desperate, weak, and dependent; and only by His strength can we do anything at all.

God wastes no time in educating His creatures; all we need to do is pause and ponder what lesson He is teaching us today. Could it be that God is teaching us a valuable lesson through the reality that the human body becomes weaker with time? When we are born, we are both weak and dependent. When we are old, we become both weak and dependent. Yet the life between birth and old age is our prime in which we thrive. Men believe they are invincible, and women believe they are beautiful. We are in the prime of life, and we never stop to ponder our mortality. Young men walk around with puffed-up and cocky attitudes. They believe that they can conquer the world; or, at the very least, they want people to believe that about them.

I find it interesting that no matter what the social class is, people act the same way. Some want to show strength in their wealth; others want to show strength in their intimidating appearances. Some take pride in their nice clothes, while others take pride in marking their bodies with tattoos. Some want to show their contribution to the world by living in a tiny home, while others want to show their achievements by owning a mansion. There are those in the middle who believe both sides are wrong. All people believe they are right. People believe that the opposite lifestyle either looks down on or envies them, but they fail to realize the frailty of life.

I was in Las Vegas once and noticed the way people were carrying themselves, as though they wanted everyone around them to believe they were something special. I remember thinking, as I watched a young man calling attention to himself by his appearance, that the people who were looking at him today would forget about him tomorrow. I remember young ladies calling attention to their bodies, believing that their beauty was their contribution to the world. Each woman wanted to be more attractive than the others. Each man wanted to be more powerful, more intimidating, or more highly regarded than the others. I remember other people slithering through the darkness, wanting to disappear because they had lost hope. They had realized that their cry for attention was never heard. People did not think of their mortality or eternity. No one was giving any thought to the Source of Life that gave them energy to sin—to sin against the very Source of Life Himself. If only they understood the Source of Life, if only they understood that that Source made a way to have eternal life, if only they understood that the very Creator died for them so they could have real life, and if only they understood the gospel and believed with fear and trembling, they truly would be something special. They would be children of the King. This possibility will never be realized if people live as if the illusion that strength is found within themselves is real.

The time between birth and old age is an opportunity to learn a valuable lesson. It is easy when we are old to look back and see how the years click by like the second hands on clocks. When we are young, we understand that we will not live forever; yet we live as though we will. We put off until tomorrow what could be done today. Most people want to leave a mark, to be remembered, or to leave behind a legacy. Some people don't care if it is a good mark or a bad mark; they just want to be remembered. What if we learned, between birth and old age, what our bodies teach us as we grow old? What if we learned that we are weak, mortal creatures who are dependent on God for our very existence? What if we learned that in our weakness, we find true purpose? What if we understood that in our weakness, we find true strength—His strength? Would that change the way we live? Would that change the way we treat each other and the way we serve God?

Heraclitus, a Greek pre-Socratic philosopher, is famous for saying, "The same man cannot step into the same river twice." Heraclitus could see the years ticking away like the second hand on a clock. He could see the drops that made up the river moving quickly downstream, never to return. He understood that the man had changed in the seconds it took him to step into the river and that the droplets of water that made up the river had moved on and had no control to stay in place. Yet he never connected what he saw to the important lesson that he needed to learn—that of faith.

We serve a God Who isn't like us. While we are mortal, God is immortal. While we are finite, God is infinite. While we are mutable, God is immutable. While we are weak and dependent, God is omnipotent. The attribute of immutability is difficult for us to understand as mutable creatures. We shift and turn and move from year to year and from day to day, yet God remains unchanged and incapable of change. If God were capable of change, that would mean that He was not perfect. Change shows weakness, imperfection, and mortality. Perfection cannot change. Understanding this sets the stage for understanding why weakness is important.

We change our minds because we make mistakes; God does not change His mind or make mistakes. We change with age because of sin and death;

God does not change, sin, or die. We change the way we think because our thoughts are wrong; God does not change His thoughts or err. We break our promises because we are fallen humans. God is not a fallen human, and God never breaks His promises. I am once again talking about the source. If we understand where our ability to do anything comes from, we will understand that we are dim reflections of the Ultimate Source of our ability. We are the weak who hate the essence of what we are.

Yet when we understand the Source of our strength, we can, for the first time, begin to grow because our premise is correct. Our starting point is in its proper place. When we believe ourselves to be strong and our starting point is to build upon the strength we possess, our starting point is incorrect. For that reason, our efforts are futile. But when we understand that we are weak and pitiful, yet God has given us a mission and the ability to accomplish that mission, then we will prosper. Not only that but we will also avoid learning painful lessons along the way as God corrects us. God's will shall be accomplished in all things. We will either start from the correct line and be blessed along the way, or we will start from the middle and be chastised and corrected along the way.

Another important lesson to learn is that there are no strong individuals. There are no Nietzschean supermen who can stand alone. We are part of a collective and were designed to work with other parts of the body of Christ. It is easy to fall into an individualistic Christianity because we all grow at different times, at different paces, and in different ways. We should focus on our own growth, yet we must also understand that our growth isn't only for us to be better individually but also to be better collectively. Understanding this reality will change the depth of your maturity and the way you act as a mature person. Individually, when you realize that you are weak and dependent, when you realize the power on which you depend comes from God Himself, you begin to grow as an individual. But your growth is limited if it stops at the individual level. Strength is birthed in realizing your weakness, realizing your source of strength, realizing the purpose of your mission, and realizing you're a part of a body, then leaning fully and most assuredly upon God.

I am not promoting passivism. I realize that there is a knife's edge in that statement. We are passive in our justification, as Luther so brilliantly describes. Yet we are not passive in other areas, such as sanctification. That is the other edge of the knife because sanctification is monergistic. Monergism, by definition, means that God does all the work. Yet we are also active in our sanctification. Some would say, "Then sanctification is synergistic, if we are not passive but active." But that is a failure to understand the difference between passivism and synergism. We are active in sanctification, yet we are not working alongside God as He is working. Sanctification is monergistic in the sense that God has already determined the path of our sanctification—the course it will follow—and all we do is follow the course (by being obedient) and watch sanctification happen. We are walking on the path of obedience He has set before us. He set it out before us before time began, and He revealed it to us in Scripture. We don't cooperate with God in deciding what we do as part of our sanctification or help Him plan out our lives. We are either obedient to walking (active) the path already laid out (passive) in Scripture, or we are not. We either partake in God's will or we turn and go the wrong way.

I am speaking about the will of God. God has different types of wills in Scripture, and we would be wise to understand their differences. In theology, we make a distinction between God's decretive, preceptive, permissive, and dispositional will. This book is not about each of these (refer to *Huskey's Study Notes on the Attributes of God*), but I want to bring up God's permissive will.[95] When we refer to God's permissive will, it is an extension of His preceptive will. His preceptive will simply refers to God's commands that can be

---

95 Michael Huskey, *Huskey's Study Notes on the Attributes of God* (Montrose: Self-published, 2021).

perceived by natural and canonical revelation—put simply, God's law that is both revealed in Scripture as well as written on the hearts of man or God's commands that can be perceived in nature and Scripture. God's preceptive will can only be disobeyed according to His ordination. In other words, God must ordain that you can be disobedient, or you wouldn't be able to be disobedient. That doesn't make God the Author of evil; instead, it elevates our understanding of His sovereignty. God, in His sovereignty, gives us the ability to be disobedient; but He does not make us disobey. God could stop you from sinning—He could stop your heart if He wanted to—so He must be permissive in allowing you to be disobedient.

I say all that to back up the prior point that sanctification is active yet not synergistic. If God gives us permission by ordaining that we can actively disobey, then likewise, we must be active in our obedience. We must also understand that we are being obedient to the things God has set before us before we were born. This is why dependence and weakness go hand in hand. We are dependent on God's providence to push or draw us. We are weak and incapable on our own and must do all things through the power of Christ who strengthens us and by the indwelling Holy Spirit. The Holy Spirit will not wrestle and overpower you if you are walking in your own strength unless He chooses to, but that is outside of the normal ways in which He works. When He works through you, recognize Him for that work and be grateful rather than believe you are something great.

> Because of the surpassing greatness of the revelations, for this reason, to keep me from exalting myself, there was given me a thorn in the flesh, a messenger of Satan to torment me—to keep me from exalting myself! Concerning this I implored the Lord three times that it might leave me. And He has said to me, "My grace is sufficient for you, for power is perfected in weakness." Most gladly, therefore, I will rather boast about my weaknesses, so that the power of Christ may dwell in me. Therefore I am well content with weaknesses, with insults, with distresses,

with persecutions, with difficulties, for Christ's sake; for when I am weak, then I am strong.[96]

Because of all the amazing work that God was doing through Paul, Paul was prone to start believing he was something special. That is human nature, and Paul is just like us—human. God gave him "a thorn in the flesh" to keep him "from exalting" himself, to enable him to understand his weakness. Paul asked God to remove it, but God said no. God told Paul, "My grace is sufficient for you, for power is perfected in weakness." If we could get our heads wrapped around this truth, what amazing things would God accomplish through us? It is His power, not ours. It is His work, not ours. It is His mission; He simply uses weak people to accomplish it. His strength, His power, His work, and His mission are perfected in our weakness. Paul boasted about that. He boasted in his weakness "so that the power of Christ would dwell in him." Let us live in weakness.

CHAPTER 10
OBLIGATIONS OF LEADERSHIP IN THE HOME: A DEDICATION TO MY SONS

"The Lord bless you, and keep you; the Lord make His face shine on you,
And be gracious to you; the Lord lift up his countenance on you, And give you peace."

Numbers 6:24-26

God, Whose counsel is always wisest, has been gracious enough to leave us with instructions as to how to be godly leaders. Godly leadership must start in the home. We cannot lead in the church if we have not been faithful to lead in the home. Of course, I am speaking to men. I understand that not all households have Christian men. There are tragedies that happen. There are Christian women who were saved after being married to a non-Christian man. There are several reasons why a household might need to be led by a Christian woman. But I will focus on men, as that is the calling of all men God has saved: to be leaders in their homes. I will address this topic as though I am speaking directly to my two sons, and I hope that you will learn from my treatment of this subject.

A godly man must align his priorities, and his priorities should look very different from what are perceived as the priorities of a good man in a secular culture and family. Our first priority as godly men cannot be work. It cannot be our children or even our wives. The godly man's first priority must be God. I should be careful about how I proceed here, because some men spend all their time doing ministry and neglecting their families. The truth is that such behavior isn't putting God first. It is being reckless and careless in response to the instruction that He has given to be faithful in the family. As Paul asked, "But if a man does not know how to manage his own household, how will he take care of the church of God?"[97] Paul further warned, "But if anyone does not provide for his own, and especially for those of his household, he has denied the faith and is worse than an unbeliever."[98] To put God first is not to neglect all else. To put God first is to love, care for, and disciple the people He has put you in charge of leading, and that begins in the home.

There are things that you know to do as godly men, and I will not beat you over the brow by calling you failures. It is my intention to encourage you in the things you already understand and to challenge you in ways that you may not have thought of. You know that you are to pray for your families. You know that you are to love, to comfort, to cherish, to disciple, to provide for, and to protect them. Men seem to pick one or two of these things to focus on, and then the preacher stands in the pulpit on Father's Day and proceeds to tell them they have failed at all the rest. Why is he so hard on the fathers on Father's Day and so kind to the mothers on Mother's Day, anyway? Because you're not supposed to be a wimp—that is why. But it is hard to avoid being a wimp in a society that seems to be offended by anything and everything. People reading this book probably do not fall into that category because you are still reading, and this is meant to be a challenging book. But you must not fall into the mindset of the offended, or you will never be humble enough to grow in these areas. "Whoever loves discipline loves knowledge, but he who hates reproof is stupid."[99]

---

97   1 Timothy 3:5
98   1 Timothy 5:8
99   Proverbs 12:1

To lead your family is to love your family. Though that may seem obvious, it should be stated due to the attack on masculinity from society today. It is apparent that masculinity is being attacked from every source imaginable, not only from women but also from men who despise masculinity either because they have bought into feminism or because they do not associate masculinity with qualities like kindness or gentleness, which reflect the character of Christ. Most of the protagonists on television and in the movies are now female. When you have a male protagonist, he is often made to be a fool and/or insecure. When a man exerts too much masculinity, he is told that he needs to embrace his feminine side.

God made us different for a purpose. The man is incomplete without the woman. The woman is incomplete without the man. The rejection of this God-given design is an attack from Satan himself. To love your family, you must embrace the role He has placed upon you. This role must be embraced humbly, wisely, and lovingly. A man is not to lead by domination but to lead as Christ leads His Church. Jesus is our Example in leadership. Jesus is our Example of how to love. That is why the goal of this book is to direct all things to Christ. This is one of the ways a man loves—by being who God has made him to be as a servant of his family.

A godly man disciples his family. Proper discipleship involves daily Scripture reading, proper hermeneutics, and showing how all things point to Jesus and the gospel of our Lord. There is a failure in the pulpit today that trickles down to the family. I am speaking of a failure regarding the treatment of Christ, the Object of Scripture. Many Bible studies and sermons are all about the Christian life instead of the Christ Who gives life. Be intentional about reading Scripture on your own and learn to point everyone and connect everything to Jesus. Be intentional about taking what you learn and sitting down with your family to read and to teach what Scripture is teaching you. You cannot teach what you do not understand or what you do not know.

Our faith isn't that of the lazy person but that of the enthusiastic, driven, and passionate person. So learn, grow, and love God with your whole mind as well as your whole heart, as Christ commands. Open the systematic theology book. Open the historical theology book. Turn on the podcast, the video, or any proper source you can find that helps you to continue your education in our Lord. Compare all things to Scripture, and then instruct your family. If you have no family, do this for yourself so that you can instruct someone else. We are all priests according to Scripture, although we serve our High Priest, Christ. The role of priest reflects our privileged status as heirs to the kingdom of God. Disciple your family in this manner, as someone who is an accepted and privileged son of the Most High.

Don't be carried off by the wind of doctrinal change. Our faith is ancient; it has existed from the beginning of time and will last till the end of time. Be amazed that you have been given the gift of being a part of something so great and fantastic. There is nothing new to learn that has not already been discovered by those who came before us, and that is really a thing of beauty. Don't be destined to repeat the same mistakes our forefathers made or had to deal with. Be educated about the past. Be a student. Be a teacher. To be a good teacher is to be the greatest student. You will learn that our faith never changes. Society and worldviews change; but Christians stand firm, fixed in their countenance, stature, and direction. We do not bend. We do not relent. We do not assimilate. We belong to God. We are His, and we are to be faithful in all that we are in Christ.

We are to be content. We are not to be content in ourselves but content in Christ, much like the Puritan view of contentment. Jeremiah Burroughs said:

> Many men and women have such a natural quietness of spirit and such a bodily constitution that you seldom find them disquieted. Now, mark these people and you will see that they are likewise of a very dull spirit in any good matter; they have no quickness nor liveliness of spirit in such matters either. But

where contentment of heart springs from grace, the heart is very quick and lively in the service of God. Yea, the more any gracious heart can bring itself to be in a contented disposition, the more fit it is for any service of God. It is very active and lively, not dull, in the services of God. And just as a contented heart is very active and busy in the work of God, so he is very active and busy in sanctifying God's name in the affliction that befalls him.[100]

As you can see, the Puritan view of contentment is different from what is talked about today. Today, we are told not to be content in our faith because the idea of contentment today is that of being idle. The Puritan view, however, is that of being active. The Puritan view is that the Christian is fully satisfied in, and only in, Christ. We find all meaning to our existence in Him. There is nothing outside of Christ that we should grasp for if we believe fulfillment is found in that object. The important thing to note here is what comes after the word "if." So, in other words, some desires are not sinful, and those are okay and right to pursue. But what can make a desire sinful is believing that we will find true fulfillment in obtaining whatever that desire is, when, in reality, true and everlasting fulfillment can only be found in Christ.

There are temporal desires that are okay if they are not sinful, but we must recognize just that: they are temporal (relating to this earthly life rather than to eternity). Being content does not mean "quietness of spirit," as Burroughs reminds us. A content person isn't someone who shrinks back from difficulty or obligation but someone who faces these with a grace that is provided by God. Learn to be content in the right way—the Puritan way. Always have an active contentment in your faith and thank God that, with your contentment, He provides rest, peace, hope, and assurance.

We never really own anything in this life. I am speaking of tangible physical things. We have only been leased anything that we possess by God

---

100 Jeremiah Burroughs, *The Rare Jewel of Christian Contentment* (Carlisle: Banner of Truth, 2022), 17.

Himself. If we understand this, we take less pleasure in the gift and find more pleasure in the Gift-giver. God has given us things that are far greater than any tangible, physical things of this earth can offer. He has given us forgiveness, grace, mercy, redemption, adoption, and everlasting life. Those are the things we should take pleasure in because those things will never be taken away. This is God's universe. He is gracious to allow us to enjoy things in life such as money, land, and other possessions. In the end, we are taken away from our possessions and into the arms of our Lord. In the end, all things will burn up and will be consumed because the world that exists now was never meant to be permanent.

"For here we do not have a lasting city, but we are seeking the city which is to come," as the writer to the Hebrews says.[101] Fix your eyes on the city which is to come—the Kingdom of God. We should live our lives with the understanding that everything we have will be gone one day. What is of utmost importance are the things which are unseen today but which will be seen one day—the important day. I love the old hymn, "This World Is Not My Home." There comes a time in the lives of all believers that this song resonates with them. We can no longer feel comfortable here because this world, as it is now, is not our true home. Yet God is the one who calls us when our time comes. In the meantime, we are to stay on mission, and that mission isn't about collecting more tangible, physical things. It is about Christ and the things that are eternal.

A godly man values human life. Life is a gift of God. We have no sovereignty here or anywhere else. God is the Issuer of life, no matter what the circumstances of that life are. This is why murder is a sin. Murder is believing oneself to be sovereign over a life that God has graciously given, whether that life is in the womb or in the world. To commit murder is to destroy an image-bearer of our very God. Is a person more valuable than an animal? This question has been polled, and the results depend on what a person thinks

101 Hebrews 13:14

the meaning of life is. Overwhelmingly, the answer is that human life is not more important than animal life. Is the value of life determined by some benefit derived from it to another individual or to society, or is the value of life given by God Himself?

Animal life is important. We should be responsible in overseeing what God has entrusted to us. Nevertheless, animals are not given the same value as people by God in the Scriptures. God made animals to be resources to us, just like other resources He has given us. We are to steward these things well. It is tragic when people see no difference between the value of humans and animals. This has atheism at its source and root. In the atheistic mind, life ends at death; and there is nothing more. There is no true purpose in life. That lack of purpose brings about a sense of hopeless ambition to achieve whatever apex can be reached despite the consequences. Yet contrary to what we as humans expect, all achievements lead to despair because their rewards do not last.

For the atheist, life is fundamentally pointless; so the highest achievement is whatever can be acquired before death. Atheism is a miserable existence but is embraced because people love their sin. It is the reason human life has lost its luster. But to the godly man, life is precious because it is from God. God has made no mistakes; and if you have life, you have purpose, which is found in Him and in obedience to Him. Until He removes that life from you, glorify God with every breath. Be driven by His purposes, which can be found by reading Scripture. Be driven by showing your family (and anyone who will listen) the grace that God has bestowed upon you through His Son, Jesus Christ.

A godly man values relationships. There are two types of men—those who are introverts and those who are extroverts. Introverts have difficulty developing relationships; yet when they do, the relationship typically is deep. Extroverts have no difficulty at all having relationships, yet they struggle with meaningful and deeper developments of those relationships. God has designed us to function best when we have people that we can confide in, people we can trust and go to for counsel, and people we can help (and who can help us). That is what the family of God is all about. In the book of Acts, we get a glimpse of the way Christian relationships should be:

> They were continually devoting themselves to the apostles' teaching and to fellowship, to the breaking of bread and to prayer. Everyone kept feeling a sense of awe; and many wonders and signs were taking place through the apostles. And all those who had believed were together and had all things in common; and they began selling their property and possessions and were sharing them with all, as anyone might have need. Day by day continuing with one mind in the temple, and breaking bread from house to house, they were taking their meals together with gladness and sincerity of heart, praising God and having favor with all the people. And the Lord was adding to their number day by day those who were being saved.[102]

Though it is good to befriend every Christian that you possibly can, it is especially important to seek out (and be) a certain type of friend—one who has God's gift of wisdom. I am not talking about a spiritual gift of wisdom but the wisdom that God gives to those who ask.[103] Grow in wisdom so that you can be that friend to someone. Seek the person who has already been given wisdom so that you can learn. Don't settle for shallow relationships but be intentional about achieving fellowship or *koinonia*. The definition of the word "fellowship" today has been changed to a mindless kind of hanging out. But the Greek word that "fellowship" was translated from is *koinonia,* which has a deeper meaning. *Koinonia* means having partnership by participating in (literally social intercourse) an activity with purpose.[104] It isn't hanging out, sharing a meal together, or putting on some social event in the name of Christ. *Koinonia* is participating in something shared together with a goal in mind. The goal of course is Christ.

---

102 Acts 2:42-47
103 1 Corinthians 12:8; James 1:5
104 Strong, *Concise Dictionary,* 42

Christ is our Common Ground. There is no *koinonia* if we are not pointing our gathering to Jesus. Seek not the shallow relationship but the one in which the main reasons for the bond are the things pertaining to God.

A godly man prays. John Calvin is a great resource for guidance about prayer.

> Wherefore, although it is true that while we are listless or insensible to our wretchedness, He wakes and watches for us, and sometimes even assists us unasked; it is very much for our interest to be constantly supplicating Him; first, that our heart may always be inflamed with a serious and ardent desire of seeking, loving, and serving Him, while we accustom ourselves to have recourse to Him as a sacred anchor in every necessity; secondly, that no desires, no longing whatever, of which we are ashamed to make Him the witness, may enter our minds, while we learn to place all our wishes in His sight, and thus pour out our heart before Him; and, lastly, that we may be prepared to receive all His benefits with true gratitude and thanksgiving, while our prayers remind us that they proceed from His hand. Moreover, having obtained what we asked, being persuaded that He has answered our prayers, we are led to long more earnestly for His favor, and at the same time have greater pleasure in welcoming the blessings which we perceive to have been obtained by our prayers.[105]

Prayer is such a vital part of our faith. It is, in fact, impossible for the Christian to go through life without prayer. Prayer boils up within us and must be directed to God. It is a privilege to approach Him. Approach Him knowing that He is holy. Approach Him with reverence and respect. Approach Him with fear, but know that He loves you.

A godly man is not a coward. "But for the cowardly and unbelieving and abominable and murderers and immoral persons and sorcerers and idolaters and all liars, their part will be in the lake that burns with fire and brimstone,

---

105 Calvin, *Institutes of the Christian Religion*, 564-565.

which is the second death."[106] There is a reason God has placed in the man a tendency toward violence, although sin has corrupted its purpose. When I was a S.W.A.T. officer, we constantly heard three words: "violence of action." That is what I am speaking of. If we understand all the things we have talked about in this book, including that we are wretched, weak, dependent, and should seek humility and that God is the Hero, then we should be brave because of that understanding.

All Christian doctrine is birthed from the gospel, which is communicated in Scripture; and we find in Scripture that cowardice is equal to murder, immorality, and sorcery. We must have a violence of action, an intensity, in our faith. That intensity includes a fire within us that incites us to share the gospel. It includes a selfless defense of our families in spiritual warfare—both immediate physical and extended Christian families. One of God's communicable attributes is justice. Justice must be embraced and central in our presentation of the gospel. Justice must be embraced when we stand in defense of the things of God and the family of God. God is our Source; and He has commanded us not to be cowardly in our walk, faith, families, and sufferings. There must be a violence of action—not one birthed in arrogance but one birthed in obedience and necessity.

It is necessary that we stand strong, as soldiers at war, because Satan and his armies march against us. We are given strength by the Omnipotent One, and it is He Who stands beside us. Take refuge in Him and be strong in that refuge. I have hammered the fact that we are not to be strong and courageous in and of ourselves to get to this point. We are to be strong in Him and because of Him. We are courageous in Christ; and outside of Him, courage is a delusion. You are a Christian; therefore, you should act like one. Know the One in Whom you stand and for what purposes you stand.

---

106 Revelation 21:8

Our premise must not be strength but weakness. You cannot understand strength if you do not first understand weakness. Understanding strength without first understanding weakness will only lead to tyranny. Understand your weakness. Understand His strength. Walk in the power of His will, and be bold.

> My son, if you will receive my words And treasure my commandments within you, Make your ear attentive to wisdom, Incline your heart to understanding; For if you cry for discernment, Lift your voice for understanding; If you seek her as silver And search for her as for hidden treasures; Then you will discern the fear of the Lord And discover the knowledge of God. For the Lord gives wisdom; From His mouth come knowledge and understanding. He stores up sound wisdom for the upright; He is a shield to those who walk in integrity, Guarding the paths of justice, And He preserves the way of His godly ones. Then you will discern righteousness and justice And equity and every good course. For wisdom will enter your heart And knowledge will be pleasant to your soul; Discretion will guard you, Understanding will watch over you.[107]

King Solomon gave us great advice and touched on several things that are very important for you. He touched on wisdom, understanding, the fear of the Lord, knowledge, integrity, justice, discernment, and righteousness in this short excerpt. Each of these things is so important for you to seek. You must start with knowledge. Love knowledge and always chase after it—not knowledge of this world but knowledge of higher things, of godly things. Pray that God will give you understanding of the knowledge you grow in. Understanding is the next step and takes much effort. Next, pray that God gives you wisdom. There is no greater gift than God's wisdom. You should crave it as though it is food in the wasteland. With wisdom comes discernment, and oh, how important discernment is in a church that has gone astray!

Don't be gullible but be discerning. You can grow in that discernment, and you must grow in that discernment. Solomon also touched on integrity. Integrity is the quality of doing what is right even in the dark corners where nobody can see. But One does see, and that One is God. Integrity is pleasing Him when no other person is witnessing what you are doing. Let this lead you through everything and every decision in life. You will be seen as a hater and bigot by the world, but at least you will let them know that you walk with integrity in all things. The fear of the Lord will be your fuel in seeking after each of these things. Fear God and do what is pleasing to Him. Don't be lazy but be on the frontlines. Your word is your honor and part of the legacy you will leave behind. Read the Proverbs as often as you can and learn from them.

Though we are God's workmanship, our focus should not be on our value but on His valuable work in us. That is the essence of Christianity. That is the reason God leaves us on this clump of dirt to walk as aliens and strangers. We point all things to Christ. We stand in awe of Him as He works through us. Never see any value outside of Him. We are not the object of value; He is. God loves us—know that. We love God—walk in that. Understand the order. "We love [God], because [God] first loved us."[108]

He loves the unlovable. He makes those who are His enemies into His family. He turns the wretched into the saint. He is our Source of value and the Object of our worth. Follow Him at all costs. Never look to the left or to the right—fix your eyes upon Him and run to Him. Grab others along the way and draw them with you as you run and show them His worth, His mercy, His grace, and His love. When you teach, show His value, His authority, His supremacy, and His aseity. When you learn, whether the lesson is great or poor, learn. What I mean by that is "learn from the Great Teacher what you

---

should do." Learn from the poor teacher what not to do but, in all things, learn. The greatest lesson is this—God is the Object of our value. Never forget that, and may the peace of God be with you always.

CHAPTER 11

OBLIGATIONS OF LEADERSHIP IN THE CHURCH

"Preaching is an extremely dangerous thing for both the preacher and the hearer. It is dangerous for the preacher because if he preaches another gospel, he stands condemned. If he commits a lesser crime and misinterprets the Scripture, whatever he builds upon that bad interpretation will be burned on the day of judgment as wood, hay, and stubble."[109]

We should understand that it is by the grace of God that we have been given any responsibility in His kingdom. If we are left to ourselves, we are inefficient and unqualified to teach His bride. It should be humbling that though we lack skill, purity, and the vast number of qualities required to teach the bride of Christ, we are nevertheless called. Though we can see what others may not—those things inside of ourselves that shame us—God uses imperfect and flawed humans to convey the greatest message in the history of the world. After all, it isn't our power, ability, or craftiness that changes a sinner's heart and edifies the church to carry on its mission. It is the power of God working in us and through us. This responsibility, if fully understood, would crush us. It is a manifestation of His grace that He does not thrust it upon us in one load.

---

109 Paul Washer, "A Living and Holy Sacrifice," Oct. 11, 2013, YouTube video, 1:23-1:45, https://www.youtube.com/watch?v=o6hYEqpQxds.

So we must lead through tear-bleared eyes and must learn to fully depend on God and His grace to propel us when we want to relent. Prayer and supplication together form our relief and help form the practice that helps us press on. How great and how important these things are because our fight is not against flesh and blood! The mission set before us is the single most important mission; there is no equal. So the seriousness of it should strike us and cause us to grasp all that we can of the things and responsibilities of God. Really, it is Christ Who ministers to His people; we are but the mouth, feet, and hands. This is the first thing to comprehend and the thing that humbles us. This is the reason we never add or take away from His amazing Word.

Many people enter the ministry, believing that it is only filled with positive aspects. They enter wanting to sacrifice, serve, exhort, help, and be faithful to God. Often, people are surprised when they discover they are actually ministering to sinners. People have all sorts of problems that ministers did not know until those ministers entered Christian leadership. There are people who deal with problems in their marriages, problems with their children, and problems with their finances. There are unfaithful people, promise-breaking people, sick people, suffering people, and grieving people. The list goes on and on. It is easy to get caught up in all the problems people have and let despair set in. Pastors have the hardest jobs of all because they not only deal with the issues of people but also with the issues of leaders. If you are a pastor, it is vital to be able to unplug and take time to be ministered to, to find time to focus on learning and growing, to listen to sermons from other respected pastors, to remember why you were called to be in leadership in the first place (and why you responded), and, most importantly, to spend time in prayer, laying all the people's burdens that you may have been carrying around upon God. It is easy to get so busy with doing the work of the ministry that you forget that you need to receive the work of the ministry as well.

As fellow leaders, you should encourage your pastor. Don't give him more burdens to carry. As a pastor, likewise, encourage your leaders; they are vital to your sanity because they take much of the load from you. We battle together. We fight together. We minister and serve together. Always remember those points and take the time to show appreciation for one another. Remember to do all things with love and humility. I wanted to point that out before we got into obligations of leadership in the church. We do all things with love, for the edification of the church, and for the glory of God.

We must understand who we truly are to embrace the reality of Who God is and what He has done for us. That is what each chapter of this book has attempted to help you understand. It is easy for a pastor to believe his starting point was back in seminary; but the starting point is on the battlefield, not in the training camp. Training gives you knowledge; God gives you wisdom as you learn how to apply knowledge on the battleground through experience. We are servants, not masters. We are stewards, not directors. At best, we are sinners, wretches, and fools that have been given the greatest possible responsibility and the greatest possible mission from and for our Lord. But it isn't in our sin, in our wretchedness, and in our foolishness that we speak, teach, shepherd, and lead—it is by the power of God working through us. In our sinfulness, God shows His holiness. In our wretchedness, God shows His graciousness. In our foolishness, God shows His wisdom. In our weakness, God shows His power. That truth is the case if, and only if, we remain faithful and dependent on Him and only if we maintain His course, not ours. He is our Source. He is our God. We should live to glorify Him in our families, our ministries, everything our hands touch, and everything our lips speak.

The gospel is not our diving board but the ocean we swim in. This statement is so easy to understand, yet so difficult to practice correctly. What that statement means is that the gospel isn't something we ever graduate from. Some people believe that the gospel is understood in the Church, so they focus on other things. They fail to understand that other things are meaningless outside of the gospel. Outside of the gospel, there is only God's law. Maturity must be birthed out of the gospel and cannot stand alone. The gospel is the foundation of any growth that happens to a believer, no matter what the area of growth is. These people fail to understand that the most righteous person among us needs to hear the gospel every day. Therefore, the question that should be asked is this: how do I help a believer to mature in the faith by birthing my teaching out of the gospel?

I do not understand how we have so many programs in the Church that are not birthed out of the gospel. A marriage class that has no gospel is secular, even if you bring in Scripture and say that the class is in the name of Christ. A parenting class that has no foundation—no daily foundation in the gospel—will never be rightfully understood because application will be misplaced. Our local churches have programs for addicts, programs for children, programs for grief, and programs for this, and programs for that; we have so many programs, but is the foundation of these programs the gospel? I am not saying, "Is your foundation the Bible?" I am not saying, "Do we mention Jesus every once in a while?"

The Bible and Jesus cannot be properly understood outside of the gospel. There is a verse for almost anything that you need; however, the verses of Scripture are all about Christ and His work in us, through us, and for us. A verse that does not point to Christ is a verse taken out of context. Jesus is the most famous Man to ever live, but do you know Him? A program that uses verses—that uses Jesus—but has no gospel is a failure. Jesus can be improperly taught and improperly represented. It must be understood that Jesus is the Answer to every problem or need that any Christian has today. Plainly speaking, if you have a marriage class that does not start each session with the gospel or lead to the gospel, you are beating people over the head with the law of God rather than showing that their marriages can only be made complete in Christ. If you are teaching a class to help people with addiction, it would be wise to begin each class with an overview of the gospel and then expand upon how the gospel helps the person struggling with that issue. To approach addiction without the gospel and to simply instill rules and suggestions to abide by is no different than giving law with no relief provided by the work of Christ on the sinner's behalf.

Today, many so-called Christian ministries follow the Alcoholics Anonymous teaching that a person who is once an addict is always an addict. But the gospel comes along and says, "No; you are a new creature; you have been made new in Christ Jesus. You have been indwelt by the Holy Spirit. You are no longer a sinner but a child of God, and you no longer are controlled by sin." Start there and then get into specifics that relate to your class. Obedience must be birthed out of the gospel. We understand that faith is the root and that obedience is the fruit of salvation, yet we fail to realize that the gospel is the root of everything we do in ministry. A program that is not birthed out of the gospel will not change you, except on a superficial and secular level . . . maybe. The reality is that, without the gospel, people only replace one sin with another.

Maybe we should change our approach. Maybe we have a financial adviser in a local congregation who is amazing at his job but has no understanding of the gospel; therefore, he is incapable of teaching the gospel. Is he qualified to teach a class on finance to Christ's bride? Perhaps we have a great marriage counselor who has the finest education about marriage but does not teach the gospel as the foundation of every class. Is that person qualified to teach the bride of Christ? The answer is no. I would rather have an auto mechanic who loves the gospel and teaches it in every class be the person who teaches on marriage than the finest scholar in the world on marriage who never teaches the gospel at all. This happens all too often in local congregations. It sounds good to have an expert who may or may not be a Christian teach a class on a particular topic without considering where that expert's teaching is birthed from. (It would be the best of both worlds to have an expert whose teaching comes from the Bible and springs into that topic. But all too often, that possibility is not considered.)

The law will not change you, even if you are a Christian, if you do not birth your solution from the finished work of Christ. I implore you: do not always pick the experts to teach the class if they do not understand this principle; pick the people who are wrecked, contrite, and weeping because God has done an amazing work in them. Pick the one who starts every lesson with the gospel or connects every lesson to the gospel. You cannot have a good marriage without the gospel because you will never understand, ultimately, what marriage is a picture of. You will never be a good parent outside of parenting as a response to the gospel because you will never know the reality of a perfect Father. Every law and every lesson of Scripture must be birthed from the gospel. The gospel isn't our diving board; no, the gospel is the ocean we swim in.

Relate that to being in Christ. We are submerged in Him. The more we know Him, the better fathers, mothers, sons, brothers, stewards, friends, or employees we will be. Draw near to Him, and your selfish ways will melt and fade. Cling to Him, and you will know how to be a better parent. People don't need to understand their problems in a greater way; people need to understand God in a greater way. Things naturally mend when we understand that truth. The resolution to all human problems is Christ; start with Him and have your program. Your problem is solved in Christ; teach Him and have your class. Do not only teach "be like Christ" but also teach "Christ," and change becomes natural. Teach Christ and then teach what a good marriage looks like in Him. Teach Christ and then teach what a parent looks like as an image-bearer of God. I once attended a three-day evangelism class; and in that class, the gospel was never explained one time. Christ was never the focus; the focus was schemes and methods. Be aware of such things, and be sure that what you teach is centered on the gospel.

I believe that many church programs could be eliminated and replaced with a good class on the attributes of God that is rooted in the gospel. My greatest advice is this: you should be aware; you should be careful; you should know that not everyone should teach. And if you do teach, you should center what you teach on the gospel. What you teach should focus on Christ's finished work. And if you are an elder or pastor, pick the people who tremble when they talk about Christ. Pick the people who cannot help but teach others a proper foundation because it erupts from them like a spring of water. And if you have no such people, then now you know where your discipleship should begin. Don't be guilty of malpractice. Don't prescribe a medication without the instruction of a Physician; such a prescription could be detrimental.

Growing in knowledge is a commandment for the Christian. Jesus said, "'YOU SHALL LOVE THE LORD YOUR GOD WITH ALL YOUR HEART, AND WITH ALL YOUR SOUL, AND WITH ALL YOUR MIND.'"[110] Some churches focus on the first part—loving God "with all our hearts." Some Charismatic churches focus on the second part—loving God with "all our souls." It is rare for the third part to be practiced or even taught today. We are commanded to love the Lord our God with all our minds. That means we must study Scripture, we must study theology, and we must study doctrine. Each of these is vast and difficult, but we are not called to an easy faith.

Truth is our greatest treasure on this planet. Truth is what leads us to an understanding of Christ's work. Truth is what helps us grow in our faith. Truth can never be fully comprehended in this mortal body; nevertheless, it can be comprehended to some degree, and we should chase after it, dig deep, and be desperate for its discovery more than we would be for finding gold. Learning is not complete when seminary is over. Learning is not over when you receive your master of theology. Learning never ends. Paul prays for the church at Ephesus and records these words concerning

---

110 Matthew 22:37b

what his prayer is for them: "that the God of our Lord Jesus Christ, the Father of glory, may give to you a spirit of wisdom and of revelation in the knowledge of Him."[111]

Jesus commands that we grow in knowledge, and Paul prays that we are obeying Jesus in that pursuit. Peter reminds us that God blesses us when we grow in our knowledge of God: "Grace and peace be multiplied to you in the knowledge of God and of Jesus our Lord."[112] Peter is praying that God bestows upon us more grace and more peace in the knowledge of God. In other words, if you are growing in the knowledge of God, Peter prays for you to find grace and to find peace in your pursuit. I cannot overemphasize this: we must focus on loving our Lord by desiring to know everything there is to humanly know about Him. This takes a great amount of work yet seems very little compared to the work Christ has done for us.

Refusal to care about theology and doctrine is not a badge of honor; it is the toy of fools. "The mind of the intelligent seeks knowledge, but the mouth of fools feeds on folly."[113] This refusal to care seems to be a major theme in many churches today, especially over secondary issues. Everyone holds to some kind of doctrine. Everyone is a theologian because theology is not only a study of God but also a view of God. It is your job to make sure that the doctrine your people hold to is biblical, not only concerning primary doctrines but also concerning secondary doctrines. The way that I like to approach secondary doctrines, if they are in a setting that could be controversial, is to first point out that they are indeed secondary; but nevertheless, they are important because they are found in the Word of God. Then I would go on to exposit the text and bring out those doctrines as best my understanding will allow. It is your job to make sure that the theology your people believe is accurate. We cannot be pragmatic in this area.

---

111   Ephesians 1:17
112   2 Peter 1:2
113   Proverbs 15:14

There is no place for pragmatism in God's church. The pragmatic theory of truth is an American philosophical idea that undermines Christianity. It has its roots in Darwinism and secular humanism. Today it is often called *relativism* because it rejects the notions of absolute right and wrong, absolute good and evil, and absolute truth and error and redefines these things as what is helpful and meaningful in a particular moment. In other words, pragmatism is shifting sand, changing tomorrow what was true yesterday if what was true yesterday is no longer working. According to pragmatism, right and wrong change depending on what works. Good is only good if it helps today. Evil becomes what doesn't work and changes if things that didn't work before suddenly start working.

In this kind of secular ideology, doctrine and theology are thrown out the window and replaced with methodology. Pragmatism is sometimes true because a pragmatic decision lines up with a universal law, but what is right should never be called pragmatic because that description would imply that what is right is capable of change. Pragmatism is never a philosophy the church should adopt—ever—because it undermines the absolute truth and government of God Himself. What is right is right because it is true, not because truth is practical or applicable to some situation. What is evil is evil because it is real, not because it is useless.

Doctrine affects more than what you believe; it also affects what you do. Theology enriches doctrine and corrects it. Indifference in doctrine and theology has sparked every heretical church that has ever existed, and to be heretical because of indifference is to partake in the wine of condemnation. Be diligent, be intentional, be direct, and be clear in teaching both doctrine and theology. Doctrine comes from God, and it is the height of arrogance to stray from clearly teaching it. There are two words that people run from that, instead, they should run toward: *doctrine* and *theology*. I cannot create in you a zeal for truth; the Holy Spirit must craft this zeal in your heart. I can, however, tell you what is correct and what is pleasing to Him. Never take teaching the Bride of Christ lightly. Do not be apathetic in these two areas; rather, learn to love them. Look for ways to weave both into your teaching.

I implore you, pastor and teacher and family man, to teach the Bible in an expository manner. That is the intention of God's Word—to be preached or taught book by book, verse by verse, and even word by word. Do not dare to edit God. Every word in Scripture is God breathed. Every word is "profitable for teaching, for reproof, for correction, for training in righteousness, so that the man of God may be adequate, equipped for every good work."[114] Topical sermons are fine on specific occasions, but you should make your standard that of expository preaching and teaching. I understand there is a way to preach or teach topically that is also expository. A passage should be introduced, read, explained, supported, and connected—always—to Christ. That can be done topically, and it is proper to do topical expository sermons. I believe, however, that the case can be made that our preaching and teaching should be done verse by verse walking through whole books of the Bible.

First, this type of teaching is what we find in the Old and New Testaments. Moses commanded expository teaching as far back as the Feast of Booths found in Deuteronomy: "Assemble the people, the men and the women and children and the alien who is in your town, so that they may hear and learn and fear the LORD your God, and be careful to observe all the words of this law."[115] We find another example of this type of teaching with Ezra. Ezra was a verse-by-verse kind of teacher: "Ezra opened the book in the sight of all the people for he was standing above all the people; and when he opened it, all the people stood up. Then Ezra blessed the Lord the great God. And all the people answered, "Amen, Amen!" while lifting up their hands; then they bowed low and worshiped the Lord with their faces to the ground. . . . They read from the book, from the law of God, translating to give the sense so that they understood the reading."[116]

---

114 2 Timothy 3:16a-17
115 Deuteronomy 31:12
116 Nehemiah 8:5-8

Throughout the Old and New Testaments, we see someone open the book to read and explain the text. Jesus also opened the book, explained the text, and showed how the text was fulfilled in Him.[117] One-fourth of the book of Acts is made up of sermons and exposition that carefully explain how the Old Testament points to Christ and give us additional God-breathed revelation. Even in early church writings, we can see how important expository teaching was understood to be. Take, for instance, the writing of John Chrysostom (347-407). He was a great expositor of Scripture, particularly the books of Genesis, Matthew, John, Romans, Galatians, Corinthians, Ephesians, 1 Timothy, and Titus. He wrote commentaries on these books that are known as his *Homilies*. Chrysostom writes, "For we ought to unlock the passage by first giving a clear interpretation of the words. What then does the saying mean? We must not attend to the words merely, but turn our attention to the sense, and learn the aim of the speaker, and the cause and the occasion, and by putting all these things together turn out the hidden meaning."[118] These are all the building blocks of a literal, grammatical, and historical hermeneutic. When a Bible teacher strays from this hermeneutic, his aim will be at the wrong thing.

Second, it is easier for the members of the congregation to study ahead when verse-by-verse exposition is the standard. This will help them better understand the passage and commit it to memory. Paul chastises the church at Corinth for not being able to eat solid food because they were still infants who could only drink milk.[119] Our job is to help our people to be able to eat solid food. One of the ways we do that is by enriching our people's understanding of Scripture through our daily reading of Scripture. Reading a passage, studying it, and meditating on it during the week before it is preached on Sunday morning is a fantastic way to help our people grow.

---

117   Luke 4:16-21; Luke 24:27
118   Nathan Busenitz, *Forerunners of the Faith: Teachers Guide: Thirteen Lessons to Understand and Appreciate the Basics of Church History* (Chicago: Moody Publishers, 2020), 157.
119   1 Corinthians 3:1-2

Third, the church will exposit at home the way you exposit from behind the pulpit. Many preachers and teachers today believe they must keep their message simple and free of any depth or significant meaning. They believe that the depths should be reached in small groups. However, they fail to realize that their congregations will only grow as deep as the message presented from behind the pulpit. Do not be the reason your congregation or students stay in toe-deep waters. They will rise to the level and depth of your teaching. (This ascent can often happen by a sort of purging. Sometimes, you may be confronted by a person who enjoys confrontation or who likes to play "confuse the teacher." These types of people will either wind up leaving your teaching, or they will learn to love you because of your unwavering stance. For the most part, however, people want to learn and are hungry for deep and clear teaching.) Do not feel as though you must cover more real estate and hurry through the passage. It is all the Word of God, whether you are in a book for three months or for three years. Take the time to examine everything—to explain everything. It is your responsibility to preach and teach the whole counsel of God. You will not edit God, will you?

Fourth, expository preaching forces the preacher or teacher to deal with the whole counsel of God rather than a soapbox issue or pet topic. Verse-by-verse teaching forces you to cover things that are uncomfortable. You may feel as though you may offend someone by teaching certain subjects that Scripture deals with; but as a minister, you must not remain silent about or ignorant of a particular doctrine of Scripture. If you do not understand a doctrine, this will force you to study and learn. Be careful not to be guilty of eisegesis of your subject.

Eisegesis is reading your own ideas into the text rather than drawing the true meaning out of the text as God intended. Eisegesis is so easy to do when you have a particular bias about a doctrine. To prevent eisegesis, I like to study controversial matters from the perspectives of the greatest scholars on all sides to find what the Bible says on the subject. Don't root for your favorite ball team, in other words. If you are amillennial in your theology, study the greatest scholars of dispensationalism and vice versa. If you are against Calvinism, study its greatest scholars and vice versa. Perhaps you are wrong, and your bias prevents you from seeing the truth. Perhaps you are trying to defend something God never said or a characteristic of God that is found nowhere in Scripture.

Doctrine and theology ought not to be taken lightly. If you are right, then you are better equipped. If you are wrong, then do not be afraid to admit you are wrong. You will probably learn that you have mislabeled and mistaught certain things from the other camp. Doctrine is like a drum. A drum has many lugs all around it that must be tightened to the same tension; emphasis on doctrine is similar. If you tighten one lug of a drumhead and forget the other lugs, the drum will be out of tune. Each lug must be precisely tightened, just like each doctrine of Scripture must not be emphasized over another. Don't beat an out-of-tune drum.

John MacArthur gives ten reasons why we should only be engaged in expositional preaching:

1. Expositional preaching submits the soul and the church to the authority of God and the headship of Christ.
2. Expositional preaching works in concert with the Holy Spirit to produce sanctification in the life of the believer.
3. Expositional preaching produces humility and submission in the preacher and the congregation.
4. Expositional preaching conforms the thinking of the believer to the mind of Christ.
5. Expositional preaching prioritizes the glory of God and the majesty of Christ.
6. Expositional preaching infuses the pulpit with power as the preacher conveys a divine message through the inspired Word.
7. Expositional preaching transforms lives because it's the Word.

8. Expositional preaching protects the flock of God from false teaching and error.

9. Expositional preaching produces theologically deep, humble prayer that is focused on the things of God.

10. Expositional preaching teaches God's people how to truly love the Lord and obey the first great commandment, to love the Lord God with all your heart, soul, and mind.[120]

Do you want your teaching to be remembered because of a story you told, or do you want to be remembered for unashamedly preaching the Word of God and letting the Word itself bring about conviction? Our Christian ancestors who are remembered are not those who told funny or entertaining stories but the men who persistently pressed on through entire books of Scripture without apology. John Calvin preached twice on Sunday and every weekday of every other week for over an hour and with no manuscript or notes to the tune of over two thousand sermons in twenty-five years. He preached verse by verse and book by book. His congregation even carried him into the pulpit on his deathbed because they couldn't get enough of God's Word being preached in this manner. He preached verse by verse through almost the entire New Testament and much of the Old Testament. John Wesley delivered over forty thousand sermons in his lifetime and is remembered not for his stories but for his convictions. George Whitefield preached to as many as twenty-three thousand people at one time to the tune of over thirty thousand sermons and is known for his powerful approach to Scripture, not his powerful illustrations.

Do not take on so many verses that you must summarize. Be careful not to pick out only certain themes when you are teaching a book verse by verse. I have taken notice of this in expository circles, and it leaves me wanting and

---

120 "Heading: Why Expository Preaching?" The MacArthur Center for Expository Preaching, accessed August 8, 2023, macarthurcenter.org/about/expository-preaching.

troubled. A small section of Scripture can apply to a multitude of things and is designed to do so. When you are crafting your teaching, be sure to read the text and explain it well. Make sure you point to Christ and His work as they are foreshadowed or reflected in the text. Try to bring out everything about the nature and attributes of God that is applicable to the text. Exhort your listeners to worship and praise God because of Who He is and what He has done. These simple things will help you hit the most important aspects of your section of Scripture.

"Preach as a dying man to dying men."[121] There is more to preaching than simply lecturing or proper exegesis. When you teach—when you preach—understand that you have been given authority by God and you must speak as someone who has the authority of God. Your primary concern should be to declare the truth of God, not to give your opinion. This should be done with an authoritative voice, understanding where your authority comes from. When you put together a sermon or lesson, be thinking of two additional things beyond what we have covered: how do I glorify God? How do I edify the Church? This is also true if you are teaching a small group or Sunday school class. Teach with conviction and authority. You don't have the authority to do that if your teaching is full of stories or personal examples from your own life.

Discernment has left the building in many local churches. Paul wrote to Timothy about how apostasy will be a major theme in the church in later times: "But the Spirit explicitly says that in later times some will fall away from the faith, paying attention to deceitful spirits and doctrines of demons, by means of the hypocrisy of liars seared in their own conscience as with a branding iron."[122] We are not playing games in the kingdom of God. You must be aware of the things you say in the name of God. You must compare all that is said from others to the infallible Word of God. If you drill down

---

121   Richard Baxter, *The Poetical Fragments of Richard Baxter* (London: Pickering, 1821), 40.
122   1 Timothy 4:1-2

deep enough into many problems in the church today, you will find a failure to truly hold to the sufficiency of Scripture. If the sufficiency of Scripture is given lip service yet the actions that follow a sermon say otherwise, why would you dive into the depths of Scripture? The individual is left in a haze of knowledge, and discernment becomes abstract if you are not showing people the sufficiency of Scripture.

Knowledge of the Bible, while also believing there is something more—some other great and equal truth—or that God forgot to say something, will only leave a person open to wrong ideas and wrong views of God. That person's understanding of God and the doctrines found in the Scriptures will be abstract, unclear, or hazy rather than crystal clear. God's Word is sufficient, and that truth is one of the foundations of seeing God's Word in a way that is not abstract, unclear, or hazy but perfect and understandable. God did not forget to put something in His Word. There is no equal truth that is out there floating around in the universe somewhere. To believe such a thing would be to inadvertently hold to the heretical teachings of the Gnostics, who believed that secret knowledge was required for salvation.

I am never shocked when I go to a church that is numbers-oriented, and there is no discernment. It doesn't surprise me when I hear there is no discernment from a pastor or leader that misses the gospel in every message. When I hear that churches that are focused on moralistic therapeutic deism are lacking discernment, I do not gasp in astonishment. What surprises me is when I go to an exegetical church (one in which the text of Scripture is preached verse by verse) that preaches the gospel and find a Rick Warren book. It surprises me when the leaders do not speak with two voices, as Calvin said: one to preach the Word and one to chase away wolves.[123]

Discernment not only has to do with what is said but also what is not said. Do not only listen for lessons of morality but also listen for the centrality

---

123   John Calvin, *Commentaries on the Epistles to Timothy, Titus, and Philemon*, trans. William Pringle (Edinburgh: Calvin Translation Society, 2008), 296. Internet Archive.

of Christ. When you craft a sermon or lesson, be sure to not miss its finest point: Christ. Discernment is not only a gift but also a skill that can be honed. Listen carefully when you are being taught. Be careful when you craft a lesson or sermon. Speak with two voices by pointing people to Christ and, when appropriate, pointing out heresies and false teachers. Learn and teach how to critically think and how to compare everything that is said to Scripture. It is impossible to possess discernment if you do not know Scripture.

Do not be disheartened when your church does not grow. The reality is that people want weak churches. That is why weak and heretical churches are often full—because they give people what they want. There are many false converts in America. Don't let their numbers in heretical churches make you feel as though you have failed in your ministry. God builds His church. God simply expects you to be faithful in what He has placed upon you and entrusted you with. Be focused on being faithful rather than influential, and your faithfulness may become influential by the providence of God. Take the three hundred of God's elect over the thirty-two thousand unteachable apostates. Your mission is to equip them and to edify them through sound doctrine, exposition, and deep theological teaching.

Some pastors preach only the harder things rather than preaching the harder things and the deeper things. Some pastors preach the harder things because the harder things make them feel as though they are the martyrs who embrace controversy, and they are fulfilled because of it. They find satisfaction in the conflict, yet they may fall short in the overall mission of maturity (instead of conflict) for their congregations. Make it your goal to not only awaken the senses but also to plunge the senses into the depths of Scripture. That goal is why you must be a student of theology proper for life. You must be quenched by the depths, not just the conflicts.

A good leader or elder should understand proper hermeneutics. I like to think of hermeneutics as a symphony. If you have been to a middle school band concert, you will have taken note of what I call the "squeaker"—the one who is out of tune with the rest. If you compare a middle school band to a great professional symphony, you will notice an enormous contrast. The same can be said of hermeneutics. You must take the Bible, from Genesis to Revelation, as one God-breathed book. If a verse stands out on its own and seems out of tune with the rest, the squeaker is you, not the verse. The Bible is perfect and has no contradictions. You must not forget what Scripture said on the page before. Look at the context—that is the most important thing. Look at the historical context of the passage itself and the way it has always been interpreted in church history. Look at the grammar and the original language. Look at how the verse fits into what is said overall in Scripture. This takes tremendous time and effort, but you should be motivated by remembering Whom you stand before.

A good leader or elder should take a great deal of time to understand the difference between an imperative and an indicative in Scripture. This is the thing that separates the legalist from the exegete. An imperative is a command of Scripture. An indicative is the context of the fulfillment of the command or imperative. The indicative is Christ. A law or a command is always fulfilled through Christ. Never preach or teach a law without the gospel. A proper teaching has both law and gospel weaved throughout. Never preach a command without saying that it is and showing how it is fulfilled in Jesus. He is our Hero; we are but image-bearers. We can only obey an imperative by being submerged in Him and allowing His work to burst forth from us. Remember the indicative in all your imperatives, or you will be labeled as a heretic. "Preaching without a grace focus concentrates on means of earning divine acceptance, proofs of personal righteousness, and comparisons with those less holy. Preaching with a grace focus concentrates on responding to God's mercy with loving thankfulness, joyful worship, humble service, and a caring witness to the Savior's love."[124]

---

124 Bryan Chapell, *Christ-Centered Preaching: Redeeming the Expository Sermon*, 3rd ed. (Grand Rapids: Baker Academic, 2018), 18.

I should clarify what some people may be thinking about what I have said about application—that I have been against or have downplayed the application of Scripture in this book. I am not against application; I am against poor exegesis or bringing your own ideas into a text. I believe application is a good thing if done correctly. I know what many seminaries and well-respected pastors say about application: that it should be a part of every sermon or teaching. I do not believe that is always the case. I do not believe that is always the intent of Scripture. Some portions of Scripture are, in fact, not always intended to be applied; for instance, historical narratives are merely descriptive, not prescriptive. I am not against application; I am against playing the part of the Holy Spirit in the body of Christ.

For instance, I have sat through a three-week exposition of 2 Samuel 13-15 in which the focus was entirely on application, specifically forgiveness. Second Samuel is about more than forgiveness; so when the entirety of the exposition was directed toward forgiveness, bad exegesis was the result. It would have been better to exposit the text and bring up forgiveness when appropriate within the text rather than the preacher's preferred topic of forgiveness superseding the meaning of three chapters of Scripture. There may have been listeners who needed to understand forgiveness; but there may have also been others who needed to understand leadership, stewardship, faithfulness, steadfastness, consequences, wisdom, and all these things as part of the character of Christ. Rightly exposit/explain the text and let the Holy Spirit do His work in the hearts of believers. I have witnessed many sermons where application superseded the text. It appeared that the expositor spent more time trying to come up with some application than he did properly studying what the text actually means.

We should define the word *application* and how the concept of application should properly be used in a sermon. I believe the word *application* is simply too loose of a word for most people, especially preachers of the gospel. It allows the expositor's mind to be carried off into a lawless sea if no standard has been set. I like to refer to two types of application: explicit application and implicit application. An explicit application would be an application that is both drawn from the text and that the text clearly states, or an application that is properly reached through historical-grammatical hermeneutics. An implicit application would be an application that is not found in the text or through hermeneutics but could be stacked upon or read into (not drawn from) the text. As an example, look at the story of the sacrifice of Isaac. An implicit application would be that Isaac must have felt betrayed by Abraham when he was bound for sacrifice, so let us talk about how to deal with betrayal. An explicit application would be that this text foreshadows the work of Christ. God sacrificed His only Son in our place so that we could be given eternal life.

Scripture is full of explicit application, and we should preach or teach what is presented to us by God Himself in the text we are expositing. If you are expositing a text that contains explicit application, you must fully unpack the text in the way God intended. Methods of interpretation such as implicit application outside of the text or trying to find application in a text that has no explicit application can be a real problem if the expositor is not highly skilled. In other words, only some people should teach implicit application because many people are bad at it and unconsciously play the part of the Holy Spirit. The Holy Spirit's job is to bring application to the Word of God. Again, I am not talking about texts that have application but texts that lack explicit application.

Preachers of the Word of God must be highly skilled if they want to bring application in these instances. There were great preachers of antiquity that were experts at this, such as Charles Spurgeon; but we have few Charles Spurgeons today. In most cases, especially as a new pastor or teacher, you should simply stick to explaining the text on the page you are expositing. Many times, I have witnessed expositors playing the part of the Holy Spirit by trying to bring some application that has nothing to do with the text. Perhaps this application is a soapbox issue to them, or they are trying to stick to what was taught in seminary. Do not feel like you must find some application to bring to the listener if there is none found explicitly in the text. Stick with explaining the text and let the Holy Spirit do His work in the hearts of people. If you are going to bring an application into a text that has no explicit application, bring it from other Scriptures.

Another good way of bringing an application is through church history. As an example, I like to think of Polycarp, who was a first-generation church father. In many ways he is one of my heroes that is found outside of the pages of Scripture. He was discipled by the apostle John and was the pastor of the church in Smyrna, one of the churches Jesus wrote a letter to in the book of Revelation. Some church traditions even say that Polycarp was bishop of Smyrna when the book of Revelation was written. Polycarp became a wanted man because of his unwavering stand for the truth of the gospel. His congregation warned him that Rome was coming to arrest him and that he would be killed if he did not flee the city. Polycarp refused to go; bringing the people of Smyrna the good news of Jesus Christ was worth risking his life. But his church members implored him to leave; he was too important to them. They convinced him to go, and he reluctantly fled the city.

In the meantime, Roman soldiers had captured some of his church members. The soldiers began to torture these Christians to find the location of Polycarp. Under such severe torture, they reluctantly gave up Polycarp and told the soldiers his location in the countryside. When the soldiers found him, they were reluctant to arrest him because of his age. He was an old man, and they took pity on him. Polycarp asked them if he could pray before they carried him away to the coliseum to be mocked in front of the large crowd. They allowed him to pray; and he continued for three hours, pouring out his final prayer to God—or so he thought. When they brought Polycarp into the coliseum, in front of the proconsul and the people, the proconsul also took pity on him because of his age. It would not be entertaining to kill such an old man, after all. So they told him that all he had to say was, "Away with the atheists," and they would let him go. What they were asking was for him to renounce Christ as the only way to be saved.

Most Romans believed in multiple gods; so to them, Polycarp was an atheist because he believed in only one true God and denied the existence of any others. Polycarp turned their very words against them; and motioning to the proconsul and the crowd, he said these words: "Away with the atheists." This did not go over well, yet they still did not want to kill him, for it would not be as entertaining because of his great age. So they asked him to renounce Christ. That is when he said these famous words: "Eighty and six years I have served Him and He has done me no wrong; how can I now blaspheme my Lord and Savior?" That was enough for the proconsul and the people to know where Polycarp stood, and he was burned to death.

The story of Polycarp is but an example of the countless people throughout history that have stood, by the power of the Holy Spirit, to face death and to persevere for the name of Christ. And death was given to Polycarp by being burned at the stake in front of all the people. I like to use the story of Polycarp to instill boldness and reliance on God for the edification of the church. There are countless historical narratives that can be used as sources for applications. Nevertheless, I would use them sparingly because Scripture contains many applications; you just need to know where to look.

Every text of Scripture has but one meaning, yet every text has thousands of applications. If you attempt to bring an implicit application to a text, how do you know it is effective when there are hundreds of other implicit applications for the text? Perhaps you have people in the congregation that are dealing with a dozen issues that this text could help them with, but you hit on an implicit application that misses the mark for them by not applying to any of their situations. Now they apply the application presented rather than allowing the Holy Spirit to work in their hearts through the exposition of the text. It is best to point all things to Christ as an application because that application is never implicit. I am speaking of Christocentric hermeneutics, not Christomonic hermeneutics.

We should remember that metaphorically speaking, we approach God when we assemble as a body. I say "metaphorically speaking" because God is omnipresent, but I can think of no greater words to show the seriousness of assembly. There should be a sense of awe in the house of God—a sense of respect and honor. The writer to the Hebrews described this well: "Therefore, since we receive a kingdom which cannot be shaken, let us show gratitude, by which we may offer to God an acceptable service with reverence and awe; for our God is a consuming fire."[125]

Today, we have departed from such reverence and awe. People come to church to assemble, and it feels no different than a day at the supermarket or beach. In antiquity, church buildings were built for the purpose of driving the individual into an overwhelming awareness that we have just stepped into something far greater than ourselves—an awareness that we have stepped into the holy. Today, people say, "The Church is the people, not the building." There is truth to that; but over time, this view has diminished not only our awe of God but also our awe of being a part of His body. Don't march into the church like you march into the supermarket; have some respect. You say, "Our congregation wants people to be comfortable; come as you are." I say that is true to an extent.

But for you, Christian, I encourage you to be the example that shows that God is to be feared. You are approaching a unified body of Christ in whom and through whom the Holy Spirit is active and working. As a body of Christ, you approach, in unity, to worship the One Who crushes the reprobate and crowns the elect. He is infinitely beyond a mere president or king. He is King of kings and Lord of lords. Give Him the awe and respect you will have the day you stand before Him in the throne room. Do not become too

---

125 Hebrews 12:28-29

comfortable—too numb—with His goodness, so that you do not disregard His glory.

People are hurting because life is difficult. We have sympathy for hardship and loss. We cry with our people like we celebrate with our people. We want to help; we want to be good shepherds, but we must understand that the starting point of bringing ointment to the wound is Christ. We must learn to point people to His sovereignty when things go wrong. We must learn to point people to His love and wisdom in a time of loss. His attributes are our resolutions, yet the gospel must be our foundation. A proper understanding of God's attributes comforts the believer in great times of trial and difficulty. There is nothing more comforting than knowing what He has done for us, and any child of His will never tire of that reminder. The gospel will not insult the intelligence of believers; it will enrich their reliance on Him and bring to remembrance the truth that we are a part of something much greater than ourselves. The gospel binds the individual to Christ and Christ to the people.

CONCLUSION
WHEN THE CACTUS BLOOMS

"As for me, I shall behold Your face in righteousness;
I will be satisfied with Your likeness when I awake."

Psalm 17:15

My wife and I live in one of the most beautiful places on earth—Colorado. One of our favorite times of year is spring, when the wildflowers begin to grow. They cover our property in early spring, but they never seem to last very long. In late spring, most of the wildflowers begin to die. It is a blessing to walk through the fields on top of the mesa and to appreciate the wildflowers before they are gone. But one of the most irritating things are those stupid cacti that hide as if they are waiting to be stepped on. How these little cacti make it into various areas of the body and become embedded is interesting. It is normal, when we walk the dogs, to bring along a pocketknife to dig the cactus needles out of their feet and sometimes out of their mouths after they try to bite the needles off their paws. When people visit, they are warned, when walking on the mesa, to watch for cacti; yet inevitably, they always come back telling a story about the pain they felt plucking a needle from some random place on their bodies.

These cacti are quite despised on our property. Yet just as the wildflowers begin to die, these ugly and quite annoying cacti begin to do something quite amazing. They begin to sprout; and when they bloom, they really are the most beautiful and spectacular flowers on our property. What was an ugly and irritating problem most of the year becomes something we go out of our way to see. It becomes spectacular.

As I began to walk on my property one day, I asked myself, "What lesson can I learn from this amazing transformation?" I began to think about my own depravity and the patience, grace, and work that God has developed and is developing in my own life. The more I understand God, the more I see my own depravity and His amazing work. I wasn't discouraged; I was encouraged. I was left in a state of awe and thanksgiving. Christians sometimes forget to appreciate our amazing relationship with God and fail to appreciate the great work of Christ. It is easy after years of following Christ to get so distracted bearing fruit that your awe of Him and His work begins to fade. Gratitude is the result of understanding grace. The Christian should live in a constant state of gratitude, refusing to let the sorrows of this world extinguish it.

In years of little rain, we see no flowers bloom on these cacti. These plants need both water and sunlight to produce those amazing flowers. This shows that the cacti have no power to bloom on their own. There is an outside source that causes the cacti to bloom, and there is an inside source that causes the cacti to bloom. With no rain there is no beauty. The rain is an outside source that becomes an inside source. With no sun, there are only those wicked little needles that become stuck inside everyone and everything that touches them. That is what we are without God raining His grace upon us—without the Holy Spirit making His home in us—that helps us to bloom that beautiful flower of the work of Christ in our lives.

There is no beauty in us; there is only beauty in Christ. We are valuable because of Christ in us; and apart from Him, we can only be wicked, miserable, and poor. That is why I was encouraged—because He does not leave us to ourselves with no water. We should give thanks because we do not deserve to see His work bloom in us. We were once a thorn on His brow, but that brow shed blood that brought us to life after His work was complete. And that is where beauty lies, not within this vessel but within what He does through us and in us because He has filled us and because He loves us. God is always at work, changing us, sanctifying us, and helping us to understand what our purpose is in this life. God has given us as a gift to His Son so that each Person of the Trinity may be glorified. Jesus redeems us and sanctifies us so that we can be a part of the holy family of God. The Holy Spirit continually sanctifies us in this life to bring about the fruit of our salvation so that we can be blessings to others.

That is what this last chapter is about. I am done with instruction. I am done with criticism. I just want to leave you with what you become when Christ does His amazing work in your life. We have focused on the ugly. We have focused on facing some of the problems we have in the Church today. We have looked at how the centrality of Christ is missed in many local churches. We have torn down many ideas of what the Church is about and how it should be run. This book has taken us on a journey and has slowly built a foundation. Now, let us focus on the expected results of the finer points we have covered. Let us focus on when the cactus blooms. Really, let us focus on gratitude toward the One who has given us everything.

Jesus told Nicodemus, "'Truly, truly, I say to you, unless one is born again he cannot see the kingdom of God.' Nicodemus said to Him, 'How can a man be born when he is old? He cannot enter a second time into his mother's womb and be born, can he?'"[126] Nicodemus was right; we cannot enter our mothers' wombs and be born again, and that is the point. We can do nothing; being born again is all the work of Christ. Jesus could have used any analogy, but the analogy He used was meant to drive this point home. We did nothing to be born the first time, and we do nothing to be born again. Jesus gave us life.

Our forefather, Adam, did what any of us would do with the amazing gift of life: he chose treason. God was gracious to let mankind live, but the consequence of Adam's rebellion was for us to be born condemned. We were born like the living dead because we were dead in our trespasses and sins. Jesus took our punishment upon Himself, in our place, in order that He would be just in justifying us. He gave us life; He died for us; and He reconciled us. We are born again, which is not our choice but His. Yet we are given a choice to make—that of the awakened dead. Do you say to the dead man, "Do you want life," before he is awake? No, we are awakened— we are brought to life by the gospel and the work of the Holy Spirit—and then we are presented with an irresistible gift that we gladly and graciously accept because He not only makes us an offer that we cannot refuse but also, as part of our awakening, makes us desire to accept that offer. The flower begins to bud because Christ is the rain. Can't you see His value? Does His work amaze you and bring you to tears? If we learn to set our eyes upon Him, then the trivial things we face in life are but pebbles on the highway. Our prize is Christ. What an honor and privilege to understand that not only do we have Him but also He has us.

Paul said, "I have been crucified with Christ; and it is no longer I who live, but Christ lives in me; and the life which I now live in the flesh I live by faith in the Son of God, who loved me and gave Himself up for me."[127] Paul understood his Source of Life, the great sacrifice of Christ, and the purpose for our existence. Jesus gives our lives purpose. We no longer live for something temporal and passing—we live for Someone. Though we are still in the flesh, Christ lives in us. He works in and through us to achieve His own purposes that we are the benefactors of. We receive magnificent blessings that are incomprehensible and undeserved. Our flesh constantly draws us inwardly into ourselves, so we must learn, again and again, that "it is no longer I who live, but Christ lives in me."

---

127 Galatians 2:20

Paul wrote to the Thessalonians, "Now may the God of peace Himself sanctify you entirely; and may your spirit and soul and body be preserved complete, without blame at the coming of our Lord Jesus Christ. Faithful is He who calls you, and He also will bring it to pass."[128] God is working in us, through us, and for us. This work is our progressive sanctification, which occurs as we progress in our faith and Christlikeness. We are being prepared for the coming of our Lord Jesus Christ, and His return is imminent. We should be living to do, and doing, His work as though Jesus could return today. That should bring a certain desperation to our stride as we see time becoming very short. He brings things to pass, including our reconciliation, sanctification, and glorification. Yet we should not remain passive but should be intentional and focused on our call and mission, which He has given each of us to see through till the end. Until God releases us from this earthly place, our mission must continue. Our mission is too important to God and to others for us and the ones to whom we minister to lie dormant. Swinging in a hammock is not in the future of the Christian. God calls us to retirement when He calls us home. Until then, press on because His return is imminent.

The writer to the Hebrews reminds us, "For by one offering He has perfected for all time those who are sanctified."[129] Aren't you glad that you don't have to perfect yourself? We are declared to be holy and righteous by Christ at regeneration, and we are treated by Him as if we are holy and righteous. In the sight of God, when He looks upon us, all He sees is His Son's precious blood that has covered our transgressions. He does not see our guilt and shame but Christ's imputed righteousness. He has perfected you; never forget that. You stand in His presence as a son or a daughter because He has brought you forth out of the ashes of death and into life for His glory. You were once a prodigal son (or daughter) around whom the Father wrapped the robe of righteousness to cover your filth and stench. You work out your

128 1 Thessalonians 5:23-24
129 Hebrews 10:14

salvation with fear and trembling because the good deeds you are working out of your salvation are from Him. Thank Him for what He has done. Tell others of His amazing work in you that allowed a cactus to bloom.

In Christ, for the glory of God.

Bibliography

Baxter, Richard. *The Poetical Fragments of Richard Baxter*. London: Pickering, 1821.

Brown, Michael. "Has Revival Broken Out in America?" February 13, 2023. *The Line of Fire with Michael Brown*. YouTube video. 57:31. https://www.youtube.com/watch?v=HzSg9RMthk8&t=158s

Burroughs, Jeremiah. *The Rare Jewel of Christian Contentment*. Carlisle: Banner of Truth, 2022.

Busenitz, Nathan. *Forerunners of the Faith: Teachers Guide: Thirteen Lessons to Understand and Appreciate the Basics of Church History*. Chicago: Moody Publishers, 2020.

Calvin, John. *Commentaries on the Epistles to Timothy, Titus, and Philemon*. Translated by William Pringle. Edinburgh: Calvin Translation Society, 2008. Internet Archive.

Chapell, Bryan. *Christ-Centered Preaching: Redeeming the Expository Sermon*. 3rd ed. Grand Rapids: Baker Academic, 2018.

"Heading: Why Expository Preaching?" The MacArthur Center for Expository Preaching. Accessed August 8, 2023. https://macarthurcenter.org/about/expository-preaching.

Huskey, Michael. *Huskey's Study Notes on the Attributes of God*. Montrose: Self-published, 2021.

Institutes of the Christian Religion. Translated by Henry Beveridge. Peabody: Hendrickson Publishers, 2008.

Luther, Martin. "Lectures on Galatians Chapters 1-4." In *Luther's Works*. Eds. Jaroslav Pelikan and Walter A. Hansen, 6–7. St. Louis: Concordia Publishing House, 1963.

Nietzsche, Friedrich. *Thus Spake Zarathustra*. New York City: Simon & Brown, 2018.

Orthodox Presbyterian Church. *The Westminster Confession of Faith and Catechisms with Proof Texts*. Willow Grove: Orthodox Presbyterian Church, 2007.

Oxford English Dictionary. IOS app. Version 15.12. Oxford University Press, 2025. https://apps.apple.com/us/app/oxford-english-dictionary/id978066594.

Rosebrough, Chris. "Narcigesis." December 7, 2012. Podcast, MP3 audio, 2:07:45. https://crosebrough.typepad.com/fightingforthefaith/2012/12/narcigesis.html.

Sproul, R.C. *Chosen by God*. Carol Stream: Tyndale House Publishers, 1986.

Strong, James. *A Concise Dictionary of the Words in the Greek Testament and the Hebrew Bible*. Vol. 1. The Greek Testament. Logos Bible Software.

Washer, Paul. "A Living and Holy Sacrifice." October 11, 2023, YouTube video, 44:02, https://www.youtube.com/watch?v=o6hYEqpQxds.

ABOUT THE AUTHOR

Michael Huskey is an author, preacher, and teacher of God's Word. As a former SWAT team leader, he believed he had to appear tough and invulnerable to be used by God, but God showed him that the opposite was true. Although he began to write to help himself understand Scripture in a greater way, he discovered that friends benefited from some of his work, and he now writes for their benefit and the benefit of the larger body of Christ.

Michael, his wife Nikki, and their two college-age sons live in Ridgway, Colorado.

Thank you for reading this book!

You make it possible for us to fulfill our mission, and we are grateful for your partnership.

To help further our mission, please consider leaving us a review on your social media, favorite retailer's website, Goodreads or Bookbub, or our website, and check out some of our other books on the next page!

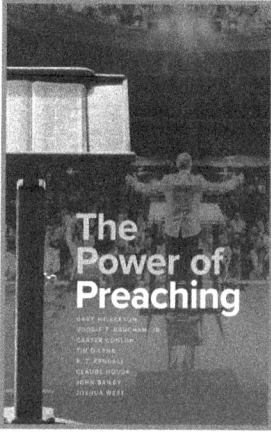

In our churches today, we have allowed ourselves to hold to a low view of God instead of seeing Him as Who He really is. And in today's world of seeking the most likes and followers, many Christian pastors and leaders are finding themselves preaching what people want to hear instead of what God wants to say. In *The Power of Preaching*, eight experienced men of God, who have stayed true to the preaching of God's Word, offer guidance on how to avoid appealing to the masses and instead encourage the reader to let God's Word speak for itself.

Pursuing biblically-driven personal growth is critical for the leader who desires to have an effective, God-centered ministry. *Becoming a Biblical Leader: 30 Days of Scriptural Principle and Spiritual Growth* beckons the reader to focus on one's calling as a biblical leader and offers thirty days of simple lessons and reflection as tools to experience the growth necessary to truly lead well.

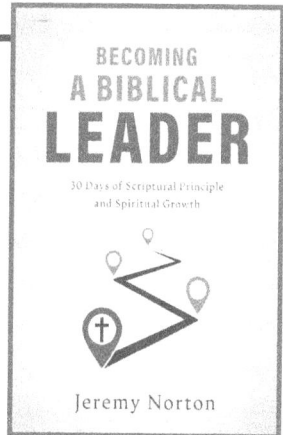

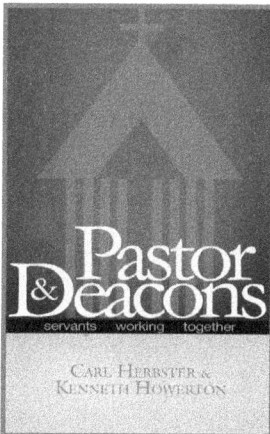

How should a church be organized? What functions do the pastors, deacons, and congregation serve? Who qualifies for the offices of pastor and deacon? How should a church manage its finances? How does a congregation biblically address problems? The authors answer these important questions and many more. *Pastor and Deacons* is a practical exposition and application of biblical principles of church organization and leadership. The "on-the-job," real-life experiences of the authors make this a particularly practical book.

www.ingramcontent.com/pod-product-compliance
Lightning Source LLC
Chambersburg PA
CBHW060350090426
42734CB00011B/2096